101 DYNAMITE QUESTIONS TO ASK AT YOUR JOB INTERVIEW

Other books by Richard Fein

Cover Letters, Cover Letters, Cover Letters (Career Press)

First Job (Wiley)

101 DYNAMITE QUESTIONS TO ASK AT YOUR JOB INTERVIEW

Richard Fein

IMPACT PUBLICATIONS
Manassas Park, VA

101 DYNAMITE QUESTIONS TO ASK AT YOUR JOB INTERVIEW

Copyright © 1996 by Richard Fein

Library of Congress Cataloging-in-Publication Data

Fein, Richard, 1946
    101 dynamite questions to ask at your job interview/Richard Fein.
        p. cm.
    Includes bibliographical references and index
    ISBN 1-57023-053-6: (alk. paper)
    1. Employment interviewing. I. Title
HF5549.5.I6F45   1996
650.14—dc20   95-46994
                                                                CIP

For information on distribution or quantity discount rates, contact the Sales Department, IMPACT PUBLICATIONS, 9104-N Manassas Drive, Manassas Park, VA 22111-5211, Tel 703/361-7300, Fax 703/335-9486. Distributed to the trade by National Book Network, 4720 Boston Way, Suite A, Lanham, MD 20706, Tel. 301/459-8696 or 800/462-6420.

Dedicated in Memory
of my cousins
Jonathan and David Green

CONTENTS

101 DYNAMITE QUESTIONS TO ASK AT YOUR JOB INTERVIEW

1

YOUR NEW JOB DEPENDS ON THE QUESTIONS YOU ASK

W hy do most employment interviewers invite the interviewee to ask questions? I have been an employment professional for fifteen years, so I do have some solidly rooted ideas about this issue. Still, I surveyed over 1,000 employers from across the country and asked them this very question. Here is what the respondents told me:

- **Evaluating Candidate's Fitness:** Over half the respondents answered that the **single most important** reason is this: The candidate's questions are a means of evaluating his/her fitness for the job.

- **Providing Information:** The next largest group of responding employers said this: They wish to provide information the interviewee wants.

- **Other reasons:** A few employers identified other reasons such as simple courtesy.

Many fine books have been written to help you answer the questions you will be asked at a job interview.

This book will help you prepare for a critical part of your interview which is often neglected: The questions **you need to ask** your interviewer. Your success in obtaining a job offer depends significantly on the quality of your questions and how you ask them.

HOW MUCH DOES IT MATTER?

Just how important are your questions in the employer's evaluation of you as a job candidate? Over half of the responding employers we surveyed said that your questions are **as important** as your answers to their questions. Most of the remaining employers said that your answers are less important, but still significant. A few said your answers are actually more important.

Employees evaluate your fitness for the job in significant part based on your questions. What do your questions say about you?

WHAT EMPLOYERS LEARN
FROM YOUR QUESTIONS

Your questions tell a lot about you. Here are some major examples:

- How seriously you are thinking about the pragmatics of the job and how well you understand what the job is about.

- What is important to you. What your expectations are.

- Your ability to connect general situations to that firm's particular reality.

- How much research you did about the company.

- Your degree of common sense; intellectual curiosity.

- Your energy level and communication skills.

- How well prepared you are (or would be in the future) for a business meeting.

- Your level of maturity (especially if you are a recent college graduate.)

Since these are the major points employers will learn from your questions, this book will show you how to ask questions which present you in the most favorable light.

ASKING IT BADLY

At the very least, your questions should avoid casting you in a negative light. Throughout this book we will give you examples of "asking it badly" so you won't shoot yourself in the foot. Here are five poison pills to avoid:

1. **Me First:** Some questions make you seem self centered. The worst offenders are those which ask about salary or fringe benefits, especially at a first interview. Hold those questions until later in the process, preferably after the job offer has been extended.

2. **Revealing Insecurities:** Most human beings feel insecure about something, but revealing a job related insecurity can really get in your way. Worst offenders in this group are questions phrased in terms of job security.

3. **Revealing Weaknesses:** Most interview books tell you how to finesse the dreaded "Tell me about your weaknesses" question. Unfortunately, many job candidates reveal their weaknesses through their questions. For example, asking "Would I have to meet a lot of deadlines?" gives the impression that you have trouble with deadlines, If so, this is not a topic you wish to initiate. If deadlines are **not** a problem, you need to ask the questions in the right way. Chapter 2 will tell you how, and the next four chapters will give you examples.

4. **Confrontational Tone:** Sometimes it is the **tone** far more than the topic which hurts a job applicant. Your tone could be a matter of your voice or of the words you choose, so you need to be careful of both. We will give you examples of asking potentially awkward questions well, and counter examples of doing it badly.

5. **Not Listening:** Sometimes people show that they just don't listen carefully. A good way to hurt yourself is by asking a question as if it is a new subject, when in fact it has already been thoroughly discussed. The right thing to do is this: **Summarize** briefly what has already been discussed on a subject. Then **ask a question** to clarify what you heard or to pursue another aspect of the topic.

"No Questions" is No Options

Asking good questions does require work. Can you politely turn down the opportunity to ask questions? Only at the peril of losing a job opportunity? Employers are nearly unanimous in saying that having no questions to ask will hurt your chances of getting a job offer.

LEARNING FROM THE INTERVIEW

This book will focus on asking questions at your job interview that will help you win the job offer. Your questions also serve a second important purpose: To help you understand the job. company and related factors better. Your questions will help you get the job offer. The answers to those questions will help you determine whether to accept the offer or not. This is an issue we deal with in Chapter 7.

YOURCO, NOWCO, FORMERCO, THEIRCO

This book actually provides you with several examples of questions you could ask, since multiple ways of asking about a topic are consistently given. To simplify the presentation, we will be using these words when appropriate:

Yourco: The generic name for the company at which you are interviewing.

Nowco: The firm where you, the interviewee, currently work.

Formerco: A firm where you worked at some time in the past.

Theirco: A firm being referred to in the third person.

This chapter focused on why employers evaluate the questions you ask them as they consider your fitness for a job. We also discussed what your questions reveal about you and how to avoid self destructive questions. In the next chapter we will look at what you should ask about and why. Chapters 3-6 presents 100 questions, plus variations, that you could ask. Chapter 7 reveals the one question you should always ask. Chapter 8 tells you how you can do some quick research to prepare the questions you should ask.

2

WHAT YOU SHOULD ASK AND WHY

In the last chapter, we saw that your questions can influence your interviewer's evaluation of you as much as your answers. In this chapter we will look at five aspects of asking questions to help you win the job offer you want.

- Achieving Two Goals With Your Questions
- Four Core Categories for Building Questions
- Five Rules for Asking a Question
- When to Ask
- Questions You Should Never Raise

Why are you going to your job interview? A savvy job applicant has two reasons:

- To get the job offer.

- To learn things you should know about the job and the company to help you evaluate the job offer.

How will your questions help achieve your goals? First, good questions demonstrate that you are sincerely and realistically motivated, well prepared and thorough. They indicate that you have some of the requisites for promotion because you have a broad and incisive perspective on critical issues. All of these are characteristics which weigh heavily in your favor when the employer determines whether or not to offer you the job. Poor questions have the opposite effect.

The second way questions help is by eliciting information you need or want from the interviewer. In general, the better the questions, the more likely you are to get an informative response.

Given your two goals, ask yourself if your prepared questions:

- Demonstrate one or more positive characteristics that the employer wants in a new employee.

- Relate to things you need to know or should want to know.

Unless your answer is "yes" to at least one of these two points, don't ask the question at your job interview.

TOPICS FOR YOUR QUESTIONS

One way to build good questions is to identify a core set of topics you could ask about. This makes the task of asking questions easier while also focusing your questions on subjects important to your interviewer. Four topics are particularly useful: the job, the company, the industry and external influences. You should prepare at least three questions for each of these categories. You probably won't have time to ask them all, but an inventory of questions assures that you won't find yourself speechless under the stress of your interview. At your interview, ask questions from at least **two** categories. Otherwise, you may be perceived as a one dimensional candidate.

Your questions about the job indicate your interest in the pragmatics of your daily life at work. There are real tasks to be done and goals to achieve, not just titles to hold and paychecks to pick-up. Let your interviewer know that you have a serious, realistic interest in the job by asking serious, realistic questions about it. Forty sample questions about the job itself are given in the next chapter.

Jobs don't exist in a vacuum. The nature of the **employing** company influences how people work there. Size, history, structure, products, goals, and culture are all important to any employee with career aspirations. What's more, every employee is part of a team working for a common cause. Your questions can show that you have an interest that goes beyond your immediate job. Further, many people view the company as a kind of extended family. If you want to join that family, be sure to ask informed questions about it. Forty questions to ask about the company are suggested in Chapter 4.

If jobs don't exist in a vacuum, neither do firms. Every company produces goods or provides services in some broader context. For example, Digital Equipment Corporation is a player in the computer industry and Hertz is a player in the car rental industry. Showing an interest in the broader industry indicates that you are thinking about the environment in which your potential new employer must operate. This broader perspective supports the case that you are promotable, a critical consideration in getting hired in the first place. Ten questions about the broader industry or profession are the focus of Chapter 5.

A particularly insightful job candidate will know something about **external influences** on the company and industry. Wouldn't you like to be evaluated as particularly insightful? External influences include technological change, government regulation and events in foreign countries. For example, events such as the collapse of the Mexican Peso or the liberation of eastern European countries from Soviet domination are likely to affect some businesses but not others. Ten questions about external influences are given in Chapter 6.

FIVE RULES FOR ASKING A QUESTION

An interview is a business meeting. You and the interviewer are meeting to determine if you are a good fit, perhaps the best fit, for the job the company wants to fill. At a business meeting, it is a good idea to **think before** you speak. This principle applies to your questions as well. There are five important rules for asking a question:

RULE #1: You Care About The Topic

If you don't care, don't ask. An insincere question undermines one of the most important bases for your success, namely the interviewers trust in your integrity as a person. However, if you do care about the subject, move on to the next rule.

RULE #2: Read About; Thought About

Make sure that you have researched the topic before you ask about it. Preparation for your interview, like preparation for any business meeting, reflects strongly on your professional competence. It also reflects on the seriousness of your interest. It is a good idea to **refer to your research** when presenting the question. The chapters which follow give numerous examples.

RULE #3: The Answer is Not Found in Some Obvious Place

You would probably feel embarrassed if you asked for information about the company's history and it is given on page two of the firm's annual report. Double check the obvious sources (annual report; recruiting literature; job description; cover story of a recent business magazine) to make sure that your question isn't already answered.

RULE #4: Barrier Free Questions

Make sure that the question you are considering doesn't raise barriers to getting the job offer. For example, let's say you ask "Is relocation a necessary part of the job?" The very question may raise doubts about your willingness to relocate. If you need to ask about this topic, preface your question with "I know that relocation is often part of a good career and I am prepared to relocate as necessary. Could you tell me how often I might be asked to relocate in a five or ten year period?"

RULE #5:   Appropriate Person

Consider your question in light of the other person's role in the firm. It makes sense to ask about strategy if you are speaking with a middle or senior level employee. Asking an entry level employee why he choose to join this firm after college is also reasonable. But reversing the questions would make little sense and might embarrass both you and the interviewer.

By following these five rules, you will present yourself as a person who is sincere, prepared and thorough. You will also get answers containing more useful questions.

WHEN SHOULD YOU ASK YOUR QUESTIONS?

Five or ten minutes before the scheduled end of your interview, you will probably be asked "Do you have any questions for me?" The previous chapter explained why you must have good questions, this chapter gave you five rules to follow and the next four chapters give you over 100 solid examples.

However, there is no need to wait until the end of the interview to ask your questions. A useful guideline is this: You can ask a question at any time if it relates to the discussion you are having. For example, let's say you have been asked to describe your computer experience. You could reasonably ask "We've been discussing my computer experience and I hope that I am addressing your questions. Could you tell me what type of computer information system is currently in use at Yourco?"

Most interviewers will appreciate questions which relate to your discussion because they foster a flow of communication. Otherwise, an interview can feel like a ping-pong match. They ask; you answer; they ask and so on. You should also remember that interviews are **stressful for the interviewer.** She must constantly ask good questions and listen carefully to the answer. When you ask a question, it lifts some of the burden of questioning from the interviewer's shoulders.

Three caveats are in order. **First**, be careful about starting the interview with your own question. Some interviewers need to ask the initial questions in order to feel in control. Therefore, prudence suggests waiting to ask questions until you have answered a few. **Second**, use your common sense. If your interviewer seems less than pleased with questions you ask without an invitation, hold them until you are asked at the latter part of your interview. **Third**, it's a good idea to explicitly link your questions with the ongoing discussion. Use an introductory phrase like: "We've been discussing widgets. I would like to clarify something you mentioned about widgets at Yourco."

"How" and "Why" Questions

Sometimes you will want to ask a question about something the interviewer has mentioned to you. You won't have time on the spot to test your question against our Five Rules. Still it is possible to frame a question that flows nicely from the discussion you are having. The key is to summarize what the interviewer said and then ask "how" and "why."

Here's an example:

"Tom, you mentioned that Yourco has decided to emphasize high quality over low cost. Why did you decide to take that approach? How is this view affecting the way you do business?"

As with all questions, be sure to ask "how" and "why" with the proper tone. A sincere desire to know the answer is positive. A confrontational or critical tone will hurt your job prospects.

QUESTIONS YOU SHOULD NEVER INITIATE

The book is dedicated to helping you ask good questions that will help you win a job offer. There are a few questions which I encourage you **not to initiate** until you have the offer in hand. These are questions which will never help you get the job, but could cost you the job offer instead.

The first category of questions not to ask deals with **compensation:** Your salary, vacation, benefits etc. This question doesn't tell anything positive about you and is premature in any event. No one has offered you the job yet, so what point does the question serve? It is not information you really need to know yet. Further, many interviewers view this question **at an interview** as a tasteless example of a self-centered attitude.

Written Questions

Some people wonder whether they should write out their questions and bring them to the interview.

- Yes, write out your questions. It will help you articulate your thoughts.

- Yes, bring them to the interview, preferably in a handy binder.

- If you feel you need to refer to your notes, say "I have written down a number of my questions. Would you mind if I refer to my notes?" Politeness doesn't go out of season.

- Don't read your questions. Just look at your notes to jog your memory. Reading your questions reduces the positive impression they can make.

On the other hand, be prepared to respond if the **interviewer initiates** the question of compensation with you. The following examples between John and an interviewer should be helpful:

Interviewer: *John, can you tell me what your salary expectations are?*

John: *I'm sure your firm is competitive in terms of salary and my expectations are in line with that.*

or

*I am expecting something between the high $40's
and the mid $50's.*

or

*That's a good question. What are you planning
to pay your best candidate?*

You can't help yourself with your answer to this question, so just try
to neutralize it by giving an appropriately unspecific response. Once the
job is offered you can negotiate compensation from a position of
strength, so try to defer any detailed discussions until then.

A **partial exception** is in the case of a commissioned rather than
salaried position. Sales jobs are a typical example. In a sales situation, the
desire to earn a high income is an unambiguous virtue. After all, the more
money you make, the more money your manager makes. Therefore, at an
interview for a sales job you could respond:

*It's hard to say how much money I would make in the first year,
but by my third year, I expect to be making at least $50,000.*

The **second** category of questions not to raise is this: Conditions of
employment which impose a **barrier** to your getting the offer. Some
examples are starting date, flex time, travel and relocation. Let's say you
ask *"Is flextime a possibility?"* The question says nothing positive about
you, so it doesn't help get the offer. On the other hand, your question
may raise doubts about your willingness to work the typical schedule. For
many jobs, that would be a barrier to your getting the offer.

Once an employer has decided that you are the right person for the
job, he is more likely to accommodate your concerns about staring dates,
work hours and perhaps even travel and relocation. These are questions
to raise **after** you have the offer in hand.

A ROGUE'S GALLERY
OF AWFUL QUESTIONS

Employers from across the country shared with me questions asked by
interviewees which **hurt** the applicant's chances for getting the job offer.
These are actual examples of awful questions I hope you will **never ask:**

- What does your company do?
- What are your psychiatric benefits?
- Are you (the interviewer) married?
- Can you guarantee me that I will still have a job a year from now?
- The job description mentions weekend work. Would I really have to do that?
- How can you determine my qualifications in a short interview?
- Do I get to keep the frequent flyer miles from my trips?
- Would anyone notice if I came in late and leave early?
- How am I as a candidate?
- What is the zodiac sign of your company's president?
- How many (put in the name of any ethnic group) do you have working here?
- Do you offer free parking?
- What does this company consider a good absenteeism record?
- What do you mean by "relocate"?
- Do you reimburse the cost of getting an MBA?
- Can you tell me about your retirement plan?

In this chapter we looked at topics you should ask about and why. We also discussed five rules for asking a question and a litmus test to determine if the question should be asked at all.

In the next five chapters we will look at 100 questions you could ask—and one question you should **always** ask.

3

THE JOB:
40 QUESTIONS
YOU COULD ASK

All your questions should show in some way that you are a high quality candidate for the job. Your questions about the job should indicate that you combine enthusiasm with a healthy dose of realism. For example, a question about skills needed to succeed will show that you are thinking about how to apply your talent to the task at hand. A question about who reports to whom can show that you are picturing yourself in the company's environment. Your questions should serve a second purpose as well: you gather more information about the job.

I strongly encourage you to ask at least two questions about the job itself. Here are forty job related topics you may wish to choose:

QUESTION 1:   Qualities for Success

Doing the job well is important to both you and Yourco. You could ask a question about the qualities necessary for success. Consider questions similar to these.

> **Q.** *When you think about people who tend to de well in this job, what kind of qualities do they typically have?*

or

> **Q.** *If you had an ideal candidate, what skills and personal qualities would that person have?*
or

> **Q.** *What would it take to exceed your expectations for this position.*

Consistent with Rule #2 (see Chapter 2) you might want to indicate that you have studied the job description as a quick preamble to your question.

> **Q.** *As I read the job description I noticed that technical skills like computer spread sheets and basic statistics were mentioned first. How significant are interpersonal skills in the mix?*

> **Hint:** Listen carefully to the response you receive. If you have the skills or qualities mentioned, you can say, "That's interesting. At Nowco I was praised for having just those skills. In fact, my communication and organization skills were the most important basis for my recent promotion."

QUESTION 2: The Near Future

When a prospective employer is considering you for a particular position she is also assessing your prospects for future promotion. If you are not promotable, you probably won't get hired in the first place. Employers don't want the difficulties caused by professionals who stagnate. Therefore, it makes sense to show an interest in career advancement with the interviewing firm.

Q. *If I perform well in this position, where could I be in three to five years?*

or

Q. *I understand that Yourco has been hiring people in this position for a number of years. Looking back at the people you hired three to five years ago, where are they now?*

Hint: Be prepared for a response which includes, "Where would you like to be in three to five years?"

Asking It Badly

Q. How long do I have to wait before I get promoted.

or

Q. My real interest in this job is to get my foot in the door with Yourco and then switch to another function. Is that possible?

QUESTION 3: Promotion From Within

The previous question asked about the **potential** for promotion. A related question deals with policy or practice.

Q. *Companies have different ways of acquiring talent. Some stress promotion from within while others are prone to look on the outside. What is the tendency at Yourco?*

Hint: You might have a follow-up question in mind. For example, "People must really appreciate promotional opportunities at Yourco. Is there a healthy competition for advancement or some tension between the appointed and the disappointed?"

If you are being considered for a managerial position, it is likely that you will have a staff reporting to you. What is the process for their promotion?

> **Q.** *I understand that there is a staff of eleven people reporting to the position we are discussing. I wonder what is in place to help them develop their careers. For example, is there a promotion from within policy?*

QUESTION 4: Training Program

> **Q.** *I read in your recruiting brochure that new employees spend five weeks in training before starting hands-on in their new job. Could you tell me more about that? I am particularly interested in knowing if the training is given by outside consultants or inside managers and if people in any given training class tend to remain identified as members of that class.*

> **Comment:**   Properly expressed, a question about the training program shows that you are thinking seriously about the early stages of your career with the new employer. By citing an interest in a specific aspect of the training, you demonstrate that you really care about the issue and that you have given it some degree of thought.

Of course, there are other questions about the training program which flow from material you have read and thought about.

> **Q.** *One of your brochures discussed an eight week training program. Can you tell me what skills we would learn during the program and would we get a functional overeview of the company at that time?*

Compare the question given here with the more typical "Tell me about your training program." Remember Rule #2—Read About; Thought About. Then you will present the question like a major leaguer, not a replacement player.

QUESTION 5: Evaluating Performance

You may want to ask how your performance will be evaluated. You certainly want to know "who, what and when," because the answer could significantly affect your future on the job. At the same time, you want to make it clear that you **welcome** evaluation rather than fear it. Keeping these points in mind, your question could be put like this:

> **Q.** *I certainly intend to work hard and prove my value to this company. If there is a formal evaluation system, are evaluations given at uniform times and would my immediate manager conduct the evaluation? What criteria are used?*

Hint: If the interviewer indicates the evaluation criteria, you could respond by saying:

> *"Those are reasonable criteria. They closely reflect the goals of the job description."*

or

> *"Those are reasonable criteria. I have succeeded in those areas in the past; I am sure I will succeed at Yourco as well."*

Hint: Whatever the response to your "Who, When, Why," accept it without argument. You can question the evaluation process in more detail if/when the job is offered. If the response troubles you make a non-descript comment like "That's interesting." It is important to avoid a contentious or argumentative tone at your interview.

QUESTION 6: What Is a Typical Week Like?

You want to make two points clear to your interviewer:

- You are interested in the nitty-gritty reality of life on the job.
- You are **not clueless** as to what that reality might be.

Combining these two objectives, you could present this question:

> **Q.** *It's in the nature of the industry and the nature of the job that there are going to be some really intense periods with long*

days and tight deadlines. Still, could you describe what a typical week or month on the job might be like?

or

Q. *If you think about your typical week at Yourco, what aspects of the job do you like most and which do you like least?*

Remember Rule #5. This question only makes sense if the other person's job is similar to the one you would be doing.

Asking It Badly

Q. What is this job really like?

QUESTION 7: Seasonality/Peak Periods

In some situations, there are predictable periods of peak activity or lulls which define the rhythm of your work life. For example, public accountants tend to be especially busy during tax season or year-end closings. Summers are often quiet by comparison. Retailers are stretched to the limit during the Christmas holiday season. Depending on their product line, Back to School clothing events or Get Ready for Summer specials may also be very intense. You want to show an understanding of the general reality, but you may have some questions about the impact on your own specific job.

Q. *The retail industry is famous for its reliance on holiday shoppers to make or break the entire year for the stores. I would be working in the customers service area, though. I would think that applications for store credit cards would increase before Christmas, and returns would peak after Christmas. Is that an accurate understanding?*

Hint: If you are not reasonably certain that your understanding is accurate, it would be better to simply ask:

Q. *I know that there are especially hectic times in the stores, for example around Christmas. I wonder if the seasons impact on the customer service people the way they do on the merchandisers.*

Asking It Badly

Q. I have a hectic evening schedule, what with aerobics and my night classes. Would you take my needs into account when it comes to busy seasons?

Remember Rule #4. Don't let your question be a barrier to getting the job offer.

QUESTION 8: Relationship to Other Functional Areas

It is to your advantage to demonstrate an interest in what's going on outside your immediate functional area. You want to be seen as a potential asset beyond your relatively narrow role.

No business today can afford to have department loyalty interfere with company goals. On the contrary, many objectives require close co-operation between engineering and marketing for example. In many firms, decisions are being made by teams composed of people from different functional areas. Therefore, your goal with this question is to show an interest in how your particular expertise combines with the work and wisdom of others to advance company goals.

Q. *I am a good engineer and I love what I do. At the same time, I realize that it doesn't make sense to develop a new widget if there's no market for it or embark on a project that absorbs too much capital. Can you tell me how the different departments at Gadgetco work together?*

or

> **Q.** *I realize it's important to have a good overview of the company as a whole. At my level, what type of working relationship would I have with people from other areas of Yourco?*

QUESTION 9: Is This Job New?

You might want to know how the job being discussed at your interview came to be available. Was someone promoted or fired? Is it a new position to address a new situation? Knowing the history of the job may help you obtain a better picture of what you might be stepping into. **Although you shouldn't mentally reject a job during the interview,** this information may help you accept or reject an offer should one be forthcoming later.

> **Q.** *Could you tell me how this position came to be open? Is this position available because of growth in the company or has someone recently left the position?*

> **Hint:** You need to modify this question if you are interviewing for an entry level position. For example, "About how long has the company been hiring recent college graduates for this position and how have the people you hired recently been working out?"

A somewhat related question would be this:

> **Q.** *Why is the position we are discussing important to Yourco?*

or

> **Q.** *In what way does this position fit into to broader plans at Yourco?*

QUESTION 10: Why Did the Previous Job Holder Leave?

The past is often prologue. Just as the interviewer will probe your past to help him/her predict the probability of your success, they can probe the job's history to help predict its potential for you.

A polite question like the following is perfectly in order:

Q. *The job we are discussing sounds very appealing. Why did the previous job holder leave?*

QUESTION 11: How Did the Interviewer's Career Develop?

Most people enjoy talking about themselves. One way to strengthen rapport with your interviewer is to ask how his or her career developed:

Q. *Can you tell me how your career has developed at Yourco? You seem so excited about this firm, I would love to hear about it.*

Hint: It is usually a good idea to follow-up on the interviewer's response. Here are some examples:

"It seems from your career path that Yourco rewards hard work and adding value to the firm. That's an important quality for me to know about."

or

"Your career has exposed you to several different aspects of the company's business. Did you plan it that way from the start or were you just ready to answer the door when opportunity knocked."

or

"Given the rapid changes taking place in the way business is done, do you think someone starting with Yourco today would have the same opportunities you did?"

Hint: Remember Rule #1: you care about the topic. Some people ask this question in a tone which suggests little real interest. Also remember Rule #5: you ask the appropriate person.

QUESTION 12: Reporting Relationships

Unless you are the sole proprietor of a business, you will probably be reporting to someone. Even the CEO has to report to someone, usually the board of directors. Asking about reporting relationships indicates that you are looking at the new job in a broader context. Also, the answer will tell you a good deal about how the business is actually managed.

Q. *Please tell me about the reporting relationships involved with this job. To whom would I report and, in turn, to whom would they report. Does everybody have one manager, or is there more of a matrix relationship?*

Hints: (1) You could follow up by asking how the reporting relationships effect the daily conduct of business. (2) Be prepared to be asked a question about reporting relationships on your current job. If you don't want to discuss your current situation, wait until you are offered the job before you ask about reporting relationships.

You might want to ask a question that asks about the significance of reporting relationships.

Q. *You explained to me earlier what the formal reporting relationships are at Yourco. Do managers tend to hold tight reins on their subordinates or is the relationship more flexible?*

Asking It Badly

You can shoot yourself in the foot by asking a good question badly. For example, "I won't have to work for someone with less education than I have, will I"? suggests that you may be bringing interpersonal problems to the job.

Remember Rule #4, Barrier Free Questions. A question which suggests an interpersonal problem is a barrier to obtaining the job offer.

QUESTION 13: Location Relationships

Many companies have more than one location. It is hardly unusual to have a headquarters in one place and widely dispersed branches or have a headquarters in one place and widely dispersed branches or divisions elsewhere. An insightful job prospect realizes that there is some official relationship involved. In addition, there may be some relationship issues which don't show up in an organizational chart. These relationships will affect your job and work life. You might want to ask a question like this if your job involves budgeting.

> **Q.** *I know from the annual report that Yourco has six divisions, but it seems that major budget decisions are made in headquarters. How does your divisional operation here work with headquarters in Cincinnati? Are managers there sensitive to your needs?*

If you are interviewing for a **sales** position, your question might be this:

> **Q.** *At what level are decisions about sales objectives made, local or corporate?*

or

> **Q.** *Do you find that the marketing people in the corporate office are usually helpful to your sales force?*

Asking It Badly

Q. Who's in charge, them or us?

QUESTION 14: Senior Managers and This Department

The company's senior managers can impact on your career and your daily work life even if you never meet them. Their impact can be felt through strategic decisions, budget priorities and work style. You may want to know how the senior managers affect your department. The answer may give you useful information. The question will show that you have done some research about the firm and are thinking about the implications of the broader picture for your specific situation.

Q. *I noticed from reading Yourco's annual report and some back press releases that the three most senior managers are engineers. Sometimes there must be differences of opinion between the engineers and the finance department. Do you have any problems getting a fair hearing for the finance point of view?*

or

Q. *I wonder to what extent senior managers invite ideas and feedback from middle managers or entry level employees.*

or

Q. *In reading about Yourco, I noticed that the senior managers are all veterans of the firm. Is that a result of company policy?*

QUESTION 15: Open Door Policy

Q. *Your recruiting brochure mentioned that this firm believes in an open door policy. Are there unwritten rules about approaching your manager or your boss's boss? It would seem that an absolutely open door could get out of hand.*

People love to have access to their boss and higher managers. It can make you feel important, that you are being heard. At the same time a perpetually open door can cause problems for your managers, like loss of time or unclear lines of authority. Knowing the real rules will help you do a better job. Asking about the policy shows that you understand how pragmatic considerations can be a bit inconsistent with the official policy. The answer will also help you learn a little about real life on the job.

QUESTION 16: Total Quality Management

Many firms today are emphasizing the need for quality performance in every aspect of their operation. This is often called Total Quality Management although other names are also in vogue. How is TQM pursued and what would your role be in that process?

Q. *I noticed some references to TQM in Yourco's annual report. Can you tell me in what way this department has been involved in the TQM effort?*

or

Q. *Is TQM an integral part of the way we work at Yourco or is it a concept to be applied after other considerations, like cost, have been taken into account.*

or

Q. *Sometimes employees get nervous about TQM because they think it might be a subterfuge to bring about staff reductions. Have there been any concerns of that nature at Yourco?*

or

Q. *Was TQM put in place by in-house people or did Yourco utilize an outside consultant?*

or

Q. *Can you tell me what the benefits of TQM have been so far? Have there ben any drawbacks*

QUESTION 17: Computers

In offices and factories, computers are a fact of life which has changed the way people work. Even if you are not working in information systems per se, the firm's computer set-up will probably affect you in some way. Your question could be presented this way:

Q. *I am used to computers from college and my present job. I wonder what type of computer information system is being used here?*

Caveat: Don't initiate a question which could lead to a discussion of your weaknesses. If you are computer shy or computer illiterate, don't raise this question yourself before the job is offered.

A corollary question would be this.

Q. *You mentioned earlier that this firm has invested heavily in upgrading its computer systems. Can you tell me how the new systems have changed the way people do their jobs or how productive they are?*

This question relates the computer question directly to your job.

Q. *I wonder if this department has been able to handle statistical work on the computer better now that you have Wizard software.*

or

Q. *The description for this position indicated that familiarity with Blossom 4,5,6 system is essential. Why was this system chosen and how has it worked out?*

WORK LIFE

QUESTION 18: Why Do People Like Working Here?

It can be a good idea to ask about the social environment related to your job. One benefit is that it gives the interviewer a chance to praise the company without exerting a lot of mental energy. A question like this one would fit the bill nicely.

Q. *You seem very enthusiastic about this company. Can you tell me some of the reasons people like working here?*

or

Q. *All the people I have spoken with seem to be proud of working for Yourco. What is it about Yourco which instills such pride?*

Hint: You could follow up on the response by saying: "This sounds like a nice place to work."

QUESTION 19: Socializing Outside of Work

A question related to the previous one would be:

Q. *I sense that people enjoy working here. Do people in the department tend to socialize outside of work?*

This question carries some caveats however. You don't want to raise a barrier to getting the job offer, remember Rule #4. Implying social expectations which are not the norm at this firm could present a problem. For example, people may socialize a lot, but you have other priorities or obligations. In that case, the response to this question may open an awkward subject. Similarly, people may **not** socialize outside of work. You don't want to imply an expectation that your job will provide your social life. Also, remember Rule #5—Appropriate Person. Asking a peer this question may make sense. Asking the CEO probably doesn't.

Asking It Badly

Q. I thought I was going to miss fraternity parties, but I notice that there are a lot of young people here. Is there any policy against office romances?

QUESTION 20: Lay-offs

Yourco may be laying off people throughout the company and still be interviewing you for a particular position. A situation like this can be awkward for you, your prospective manager and the veteran Yourco employees who remain employed there. This phenomenon is hardly unusual and you should feel free to ask about it.

Q. *While I am glad we are discussing opportunities for me at Yourco, I am aware that there have been some serious cutbacks in staffing, including reductions in this department. How do your remaining staff members feel about bringing in an outsider when some of their friends have lost their jobs?*

or

Q. *To what extent were the staff reductions in this department*

*performance based rather than a reflection of the need to cut
expenses per se?*

A question like this shows a realistic sensitivity on your part. It should
help your chances of getting the job offer and provide you with some
information you will need if you do.

Be careful not to ask this question in a poor way:

Asking It Badly

Q. Why are you interviewing me when you are
laying off other people?

QUESTION 21: Growth in Employees

The flip side of the previous question is presented when there is an
overall growth in employees. How well are the newcomers integrating
with the veterans? As the firm has grown, is the way people relate
professionally changing?

> **Q.** *It's good news when a firm is growing. There were a number
> of rough years, though, just keeping Yourco afloat. Are your
> new employees integrating well with the veterans?*

or

> **Q.** *The people who got Yourco through those tough years
> certainly deserve to be proud of their accomplishments. How
> do they feel about new employees coming in who haven't been
> through the wars, so to speak?*

or

> **Q.** *As the company gets larger, it is losing any of the "one big
> family" culture that was so noticeable in the past?*

QUESTION 22: Equal Opportunity

It is legitimate to ask about employment practices if you ask in the right way.

> **Q.** *Can you tell me how the firm's commitment to equal opportunity for women and minorities is carried out in the work place?*

Every employer wants to be known for its commitment to women and minorities for two reasons.

- It makes good business sense.
- It is the law.

Note how the question is worded here. It **assumes** the commitment rather than questioning it. Phrased this way, the question may be answered with an enthusiastic review of the firm's enlightened policies. Had you asked "Are you committed to equal opportunity . . . ", you could make the interviewer feel defensive. Further, she may feel that you are seeking some type of special consideration based on your gender or ethnic group.

Remember that equal opportunity policies can be sensitive for many people. Whether or not you are a member of a protected group, you need to be careful. No employer is interested in hiring personality conflicts or ethnic tensions.

Asking It Badly

Q. "You tell me that this firm believes in equal opportunity, but all the senior managers are white males. What kind of equal is that?"

or

Q. As a white male, will I be disadvantaged by Yourco's equal opportunity policy when it comes to promotion?

QUESTION 23: Professional Associations

You may want to ask about involvement in professional associations, particularly if your past involvement in such associations has been beneficial to your employer.

> **Q.** *Are employees encouraged to be active in professional associations?*

The answer is likely to be "yes," at least for **some** employees, since having people keep up within their profession or industry is to the firm's advantage. If you are already active in associations relevant to your new employer, mention it. If you are moving to a new industry, show interest in learning more about the associations that the new employer thinks are important:

> **Q.** *As we discussed, I like to be involved in professional associations that are important to my employer. What are the important associations from Yourco's point of view?*

WHERE WILL I BE?

Your prospective employer is evaluating you for more than just the job under discussion. He wants to assess your promotibility. For that reason, questions like the following put you in a positive light:

QUESTION 24: Future Value

> **Q.** *I plan to hit the ground running and be productive right away. But let's look down the road a little. In what way will I be more valuable to the firm at the end of my first year than I am now?*

> **Hint:** This question is particularly appropriate if you are at an early stage in your career, let's say a recent college graduate. It would be **less appropriate** for a middle or senior manager. For them, a better question would be:

> **Q.** *How will you judge my performance at the end of the first year? What qualities do you expect to see in me and what goals do you expect me to accomplish?*

QUESTIONS ABOUT THE NITTY GRITTY

It is a good idea to ask at least one question about the daily pragmatics of doing your job. The following examples should give you ideas you can apply to your own situation.

QUESTION 25: Computer v. Customer

> Q. *I am interested in knowing how much of a typical day is spent working on the computer and how much time is spent assisting customers.*

or

> Q. *I read that Yourco customers are now asked to call an 800 number rather than their local sales office when they have a service problem. How do the sales representatives keep informed so they can make sure their clients are taken care of?*

Asking It Badly

Q. Computers are OK, but I am a people person. Can I spend most of my time with people?

This question may raise a barrier for you if it indicates a strong personal preference which is inconsistent with the job.

QUESTION 26: Independent Decisions

> Q. *Can you tell me if employees in my function are encouraged to make independent decisions on daily matters which come to our attention?*

or

> Q. *I read in one of the brochures Yourco gives to clients that we promise fast and fair resolution of any problems they have*

with our products. Sometimes it isn't the product, it's the customer. In this position, would you want me to absorb the cost of some returns or repairs even if we really aren't obligated by contract?

or

Q. *In our business, you sometimes have to decide how hard to press a customer to pay their overdue bills. After all, you have a long-run interest in keeping their business. In Yourco, how do we decide about these priorities?*

QUESTION 27: In a Day's Work

Q. *You have a job which is similar to the one I hope to get. What part of the day do you find most stressful and what do you find most pleasurable?*

or

Q. *I appreciate your taking the time to be one of my interviewers this morning. Can you tell me what the rest of your day is going to be like? Since we would be in the same department, your answer would give me a sense of what my day might be in the future.*

or

Q. *You mentioned that you are going to a meeting of the Alpha team later this morning. That's a company-wide finance committee as I understand it. Do you touch base with your VP about Alpha's agenda?*

QUESTION 28: Team Work—In Principle

Many companies are emphasizing teams as a means of producing quality work at a reduced cost. The posse seems to be more in favor than the Lone Ranger. What would be your role on a team and how would team work affect your work life?

Q. *I am interested in learning more about the way people work in* *teams at Yourco. Could you tell me what teams people from this department usually work on? Who else is on the teams?*

or

Q. *Do the work teams at Yourco disband after a particular project is completed or do they stay together for an extended period of time?*

QUESTION 29: Team Work—Politics

The practical politics of your potential new job is an unwritten part of your job description. You may want to ask a question like this:

Q. *Many firms are organizing projects around teams. I am used to that from college class projects and from my summer jobs. As a practical matter, is there ever a conflict between the priorities of your own manager and the goals of the team?*

Asking It Badly

Q. With all this emphasis on teams at Yourco, how would an outstanding performer like me really stand out?

This question suggests a Me First attitude that is often a one-way ticket to the exit.

QUESTION 30: Job's Importance

You may want to ask a question which links your particular job with the business interests of the firm. A question like this one would be especially appropriate if the position's significance is not immediately obvious.

Q. *Your answers to my questions about this job have been very helpful. I understand what I would be doing, but I would like to hear more about why this position is important to Yourco.*

or

Q. *What tips can you give me for making a quick contribution to Yourco?*

or

Q. *This is a marketing driven firm. What is the significance of the finance function to meeting Yourco's objectives?*

Asking It Badly

Q. I've heard all the positives. Be honest with me, what are the negatives?

or

Do you really have to work a lot of overtime?

QUESTION 31: The Job's Negatives

Most work situations carry with them something which is potentially negative. Some people avoid asking about the down side of a job for fear of offending the interviewer. This is a needless concern. If you ask in the right way, you will actually be showing that you have a realistic outlook.

Q. *Every job has at least one element that some people won't like. In my view, that just comes with the territory. Are there any aspects of this job that you don't like, at least sometimes?*

or

Q. *If there were something about this job that you could change, what would it be?*

or

Q. *Are there any "land mines" I should be looking out for after taking on this job?*

QUESTION 32: Turnover Rates

Turnover rate is the term applied for the percentage of people who leave a job or a company within a certain period of time. This can be a sensitive question, but you should ask about it if you are concerned. There are two reasons:

- A question about turnover rates indicates that you are thinking seriously about your future with the firm.
- If the employer won't discuss the issue frankly, you may be interviewing for a job it would be better to avoid.

Q. *I know that there is some turnover in every job. Could you tell me about what percentage of the people you hired in the last three years are still with the company?*

Hint: If the turnover rate is **low** you could follow up by asking why people stay with the firm. If the rate is high, however, you could ask if this is typical for the industry. I advise you not to dwell on this issue. You can pick it up again if the job is offered to you.

QUESTION 33: Is Further Education Required?

One goal of your **answers** is to demonstrate that you have the skills need-ed to do this job well. The goal of this **question** is to indicate a readiness to undertake further education/training should this be important to your success on the job. You could phrase your question this way:

Q. *I hope you agree from what we discussed so far that I have the ability to do the job well. Do you think that some further education or training might be necessary for me to move ahead in the company?*

Hints: (1) Since your potential for promotion is part of the hiring decision, ask about success with the company, not just success on the job. (2) If the interviewer indicates the desirability of further training, you should indicate a readiness (even eagerness) to undertake the necessary steps. "You mentioned that most people in middle or upper management have earned an MBA. There are a number of good MBA programs in the area which offer evening courses. Is there any program which fits the needs of the company better than others?" (3) Leave any questions about company financial support to pay for further education until you have the job offer. (4) Listen carefully to the answer. Later it may help you decide whether you want the job if offered.

CORPORATE PHILOSOPHY AND YOUR JOB

QUESTION 34: Ethics

Businesses today are placing considerable emphasis on professional ethics. There are two main reasons.

- This is a sincere concern for proper behavior for its own sake.
- Ethics is good for business, at least from a longer term perspective.

The principle is fine. How does it work in practice? There can be ambiguities about what is ethical. Worse, you may be under pressure to do something which seems clearly unethical. How will you be protected if you blow the whistle?

> **Q.** *I was glad to read in the annual report that ethics is taken very seriously at Yourco. Can you tell me what procedure we should follow if a question about proper ethical conduct arises?*

or

> **Q.** *Let me ask you about something I hope never happens. Let's say an employee is asked by their manager to do something*

*which seems unethical. Is there an Ombudsman or similar
individual who should be contacted if the manager remains
adamant?*

QUESTION 35: Applied Philosophy

Many companies have an operating philosophy which is supposed to
guide decisions made throughout the organization. For example, a company may feel that its strategic goal is to build a loyal customer base that
will buy their product throughout a life time. That philosophy will have
far different implications than one which says "maximize profits for the
short term." How is the company's philosophy applied to your job?

> Q. *Automobile Times quoted a senior manager as saying "At
> Yourco, our goal is not simply to sell you your next car. Our
> goal is to sell you the car after that as well." How is our job
> today affected by a goal which can only be achieved years
> from now?*

or

> Q. *One of Yourco's advertising brochures states that Yourco will
> replace its product if lost or damaged. What steps do we take
> to fulfill this pledge?*

or

> Q. *One of the finance people showed me a copy of this year's
> budget policy: "A penny cut is a penny earned." Does your
> staff still have the resources it needs to do its job well?*

FIRST JOB

Most of the questions presented above would be applicable for both
seasoned professionals and first time job seekers. However, some
questions would be especially useful for recent college graduates,
particularly if the interviewer is only a few years out himself/herself.

QUESTION 36: Learned in School

> Q. *When you look back at your college experience, what did you
> learn that is helping you do your current job?*

or

Q. *In what way is this job drawing upon your college education?*

or

Q. *Is there anything you wish you had studied in college because it would help you now on the job?*

or

Q. *Was there anything about your job at Yourco which came as a surprise when you transitioned from college to corporation?*

QUESTION 37: Mentoring

Q. *What I have read about this firm is very exciting. Can you tell from your own experience if you have found a helpful mentor?*

or

Q. *I have read that Yourco has a formal mentoring system. How was your mentor chosen and how have you benefitted from your mentor so far?*

or

Q. *If you were my mentor, what kind of issues would you expect me to bring to you?*

or

Q. *Does having a mentoring relationship with one person complicate your relationship with anyone else?*

QUESTION 38: Balance in Life

Q. *As you probably remember from your college days, students have a far more flexible life than we should expect once we start a career. Have you been able to devote sufficient time to your job and still have time to enjoy your private life?*

Asking It Badly

Q. So what do you do for fun now that you are out
of college?

QUESTION 39: The Right Decision?

One way to get a good sense of how a Yourco employee feels about
his/her job is to ask a subjective question like this one.

> **Q.** *Can you tell me how you feel when you wake up to go to work
> on Monday morning? How do you feel late on Friday when
> your work week should be winding down?*

or

> **Q.** *Can you tell me what experiences you have had which con-
> vinced you your decision to come to Yourco was the right one?
> Also, have you ever had any second thoughts?*

A CALCULATED RISK

QUESTION 40: Reservations About Me

There may be occasions when you interview for a position for which you
may lack one or more of the desired characteristics. For example, you
meet the minimum requirement of a baccalaureate degree but the job
description cites a master's degree as desirable. Perhaps the description
indicates that experience in a specific industry is desired while your
experience is in another industry. Hopefully, you have had the opportunity to demonstrate that you match with the job despite lacking something the firm desires. But what if the issue of degrees or cognate
experience etc. was never raised. It may be to your advantage to put the
issue on the table. You could ask a question like one of the following:

Q. *I want to make sure that we have discussed everything that you need to know about me. Are you in any way concerned that I have not earned a master's degree?*

or

Q. . . . . *Do you have any concerns about the fact that my prior experience was in widgets rather dental care? If you do, I would like to discuss it.*

or

Q. *Is there anything more you need to know about me that we haven't yet had a chance to discuss. For example, are you concerned that I have five years of related experience, rather than the eight years or more which the job description considers desirable?*

Since the point of this question is to address unspoken doubts the interviewer may have, be prepared to discuss any concerns he or she raises. If they are not concerned about the issue(s) you raise, you could say, "I want this job and I know I could do it well. I am glad that the matter I raised with you doesn't seem to be of concern."

In this chapter we looked at forty (40) sample questions you could ask about the job. In Chapter 4, we will look at forty (40) questions you could ask about the Company.

Before you start the next chapter, look over the brief exercises on the next few pages.

Exercise 1

WHAT DOES THIS QUESTIONS TELL THE EMPLOYER ABOUT THE APPLICANT?

Look at the questions below. What does each question suggest about the job applicant?

Some Possible Characteristics to Choose From:

a. Applicant doesn't listen.

e. Hasn't read or thought about available material.

b. Excellent analytical skills.

f. Good communication skills.

c. Interested in Career Opportunities.

g. Interested in pragmatic aspects of the job.

d. Applicant is a good listener.

h. Has trouble dealing with authority figures.

Questions

1. If I prove my value to Yourco, what opportunities for advancement might be available to me in 3 to 5 years?

2. Tell me about your training program.

3. You mentioned that teamwork is critical at Yourco. Can you tell me how the teams are put together and how the Marketing department has been involved?

4. You said something about the main thrust of this organization's effort. Could you go over that again?

5. What kind of relationship exists between senior managers and middle managers when major decisions need to be made?

6. The senior managers at Yourco aren't autocratic stuffed shirts, are they?

Our Answers

1. c	2. e	3. d+g
4. a	5. g	6. h

Exercise 2

BREAKING THE RULES?

Read each question below. Does it violate any of the "Five Rules for Asking a Question." (See Chapter 2 for details).

The Five Rules For Asking a Question

Rule #1	You Care About the Topic
Rule #2	Read About, Thought About
Rule #3	The Answer is Not Found in Some Obvious Place
Rule #4	Barrier Free Questions
Rule #5	Appropriate Person

Questions

1. Would it be necessary to understand computers to do this job well?

2. Mr. Jones, you have had a long career at Yourco and now you are the Chairman. What brought you to Yourco in the first place?

3. Yourco is such an interesting name. What exactly does Yourco do?

4. What was your best selling product last year?

5. So, what's your job all about?

Our Answers

1. Yes, Rule 4   4. Yes, Rule 3

2. Yes, Rule 5   5. It depends. Rule 1 unless
                                     you really do care.

3. Yes, Rule 2

Exercise 3

QUESTIONS FROM THE JOB DESCRIPTION

Read the following job description. Then write at least three questions you would ask based on it.

Research Assistant

Yourco is a medium sized firm which manufactures both highly sophisticated commercial widgets and mundane household gadgets. The role of the research assistant is: Research computer data bases to identify potential customers. Work closely with relevant managers. Write reports for internal review. Good teamwork and analytical skills essential.

Write your questions here:

A Broad Hint

Based on just the job description, these questions from Chapter 3 would be appropriate samples to work from: Questions 8, 9, 10, 12, 17, 18, 24, 28, 29, 32, 36. For example, applying Question 17:

Q. The job description mentions researching computer databases. Can you tell me what databases you have found most helpful? Also, can you tell me what computer system I would be using?

4

THE COMPANY: 40 QUESTIONS YOU COULD ASK

KEEPING YOUR GOAL IN MIND

There are **three** basic reasons why you want to ask questions about the company which is interviewing you.

- To show your sincere interest in the firm by citing your research.
- To show that you come to a business meeting prepared.
- You show that you can relate to the company's larger picture.

You want to listen carefully to the answers you get for two reasons. First, the interview in part is a test of your ability to listen carefully and absorb what you hear. Second, the responses you get may be important to you as you determine whether you are interested in the position.

There are forty questions in this chapter. You should ask at least one or two of them at your interview.

QUESTION 41: Profit v. Market Share

Q. *A recent article in the **Wall Street Journal** suggested that it is time for firms like Yourco to be more concerned with profit margins than with market share. Do you see any signs that Yourco is shifting its priorities in that direction?*

This question indicates that you are keeping up with the business press and thinking about an issue (profit v. market share) which could profoundly influence the goals you would be asked to achieve.

A related question would be this:

Q. *I read in the **Wall Street Journal** that Yourco emphasizes market share over profit margins. Do you think stockholders will be patient enough to give this strategy time to produce anticipated profits?*

or

Q. *The **Wall Street Journal** recently had an article about Yourco and its emphasis on market share. That usually requires keeping prices relatively low to attract customers. How will Yourco respond if your competitors decide to engage in a price war?*

If the firm is publicly held, the annual report will likely indicate its structure. For example, if there is more than one division, you are likely to see that mentioned in the chairman's report on the first few pages. Alternatively, the story line in the middle of the report and/or the list of officers at the end of the report will give you this information.

QUESTION 42: The Firm's Structure

Q. *As I understand your annual report this firm has four divisions, each with a different product or service. Do you think this diversity strengthens the firm's stability? On the other hand, does it confuse the company's image in the marketplace?*

Hint: When citing the firm's annual report or other sources, be sure that the question is addressed to the appropriate person, (Rule #5), namely someone who is likely to be involved with the matter on a professional basis.

QUESTION 43: Cost Containment

You may want to relate a question on structure more directly to your own professional interest.

Q. *In your annual report, the chairman cited cost containment as a major goal for the next three years. How will that impact on the finance function?*

If cost containment is a major goal, finance people may be involved in finding lower cost ways of doing business. Outsourcing and lease/buy decisions would be examples. Of course, all departments could be affected, so there could be many related questions appropriate for you. For example:

Q. *The chairman mentioned in Yourco's annual report that cost containment will be major goal for the next three years. How much cost savings will Purchasing be expected to provide?*

or

Q. *One way firms cut costs is by better inventory control. I read in the annual report that cost cutting is a major goal for the next three years. I started thinking about just-in-time delivery systems and direct shipping from the manufacturer. Can you tell me what Yourco is considering along these lines?*

COMPETITION

QUESTION 44: Losing/Gaining Market Share

One subject you may want to get into is competition, especially with the intense competitive pressures on today's businesses. A question about market share is a good way to do that since whatever share of the market Yourco **doesn't have** competition does. Trade magazines, the business press and the *Standard & Poor's Industry Surveys* are good sources of information for this question.

> **Q.** *I read in **Soap Bubbles Monthly** that Yourco has held a 24% market share for three years now. In the meantime, Bubble Inc. has been taking shares away from the industry leader, Air Ball. What is Yourco planning to do to keep Bubble Inc. from grabbing share at your expense in the future?*

It is especially important that you have the **right attitude** and speak in the proper tone when comparing Yourco to the competition. It is fine to ask a question based on a sincere desire to understand something better. On the other hand, it is offensive to imply by your tone or wording that another firm is better than Yourco or that Yourco just doesn't understand things as well as you do. **Don't** adopt a tone like this interviewee did:

> **Q.** [Asked Poorly] *Theirco spends a lot of money in TV advertising. Shouldn't Yourco be doing that, too?*

An alternative question could link market share to your hoped-for job.

> **Q.** *If you offer me this position as branch manager, will my objective be to gain market share for Yum-Yum Cereal or will we try to solidify the base we already have?*

Notice how the question can use the phrase "we" instead of "you". If you are comfortable using the first person plural, it may make it easier for your interviewer to see you as part of the team.

QUESTION 45: Beating Firm's Competitors

Another way of showing your interest in beating Yourco's competitors is by addressing the issue directly. There are a number of ways to phrase the question, depending upon your situation.

Q. *I read that Competco is restructuring its debt load to lessen its interest payment burden. Has any thought been given to a similar approach at Yourco?*

or

Q. *Right now Yourco is marketing Magic King wrenches through its own sales force. However, Competco is gaining access to more stores by using wholesalers. Do you think their approach is giving Competco an edge?*

You can relate the question more directly to you like this:

Q. *At Formerco, I worked on a strategy which beat our competition by getting products delivered to customers sooner. Do you think that approach might boost Yourco's competitiveness as well?*

or

Q. *How is this position going to add to Yourco's competitiveness?*

QUESTION 46: Hidden Competition

We often think of competition in terms of a number of firms all making widgets and vying for essentially the same customers. Sometimes competition may be less obvious, which provides you with some possible questions.

Q. *When we think about Yourco's market, we often see this firm and two competitors. Do you think there will be hidden competition from clients attempting to provide, in-house, the same service as Yourco?*

or

Q. *BusinessWeek reported that a small firm in California is starting to make widgets from plastic instead of metal. Could* *a plastic widget become a serious competitor?*

QUESTION 47: Why Do Clients Choose this Firm?

A company's clients choose to do business with them for some reason, probably based on rational self-interest. Asking about the clients' reasons shows your interest in knowing what makes the firm successful while giving the interviewer a chance to say wonderful things about his/her company.

> **Q.** *There are a number of players in Yourco's market. Yet you have been successful in maintaining and even expending your client base. What is it about Yourco that makes customers choose you?*

> **Hint:** Be prepared to follow up on the interviewer's response. Let's say your field is customer service. If the response mentions customer service as a positive draw for business, you could say: "I am glad that a strong record of customer service is recognized by your clients. I have six years experience in the field and I would look forward to working with your customer service people at Yourco."

On the other hand, if the response **doesn't mention** customer service, you could say. "I notice that you didn't mention customer service as a current attraction to your customers. With my experience in that area, Yourco could strengthen one more avenue of appeal to customers. I would look forward to being part of that effort."

QUESTION 48: Decision Making

> **Q.** *Investor's Business Daily reported that Yourco has decided to emphasize quality service over low price for the new CopyKing machines. Why did Yourco arrive at that decision and why this approach for a **new** product rather than a more established line?*

> **Caution:** Make sure you know your facts. The second half of the question, starting with "why" makes sense only if **you know for sure** quality service is not top

priority with established lines. **Being silent makes you look smarter than being slipshod.**

The previous example dealt with **reasons** for a decision. You may want to ask about **how** decisions are made.

Q. *I would like to know something about the decision making process at Yourco. For example, when it came to the quality service emphasis for the new CopyKing machines, was there a broad discussion within the firm or was the decision left to the service managers of the copier division?*

Asking It Badly

Q. Who really makes the big decisions here?

QUESTION 49: Evolution of Business Line

Every business must produce a marketable service or product. A question about the development of a product or the evolution of a business line may elicit a picture of how the firm operates. It will also give the interviewer a chance to discuss a subject which is dear to his heart (Doesn't everyone like to talk about their summer vacation or show pictures of their growing children?).

Q. *The Robert Wrench Kit seems to have struck a responsive chord with the workshop market. How did the idea develop to package the wrenches in their own tool box?*

or

Q. *Many people were surprised to see a toy company like Yourco developing a line of personal computers. I am interested in knowing if the computer idea evolved from a toy-based project of if it came about some other way?*

QUESTION 50: What Drives the Firm?

Very often there is a key element of a firm's business that is a dominating force in how the firm operates. It might be service or quality or price among other possibilities. You could ask a question like this:

> **Q.** *Yourco is noted for refining old products or introducing new products on a continuing basis. Would you say your products are driven more by feedback from consumers or from possibilities presented by your technical research?*

or

> **Q.** *Yourco advertises "good product at a good price". In terms of internal decisions, what drives the company, price or quality?*

QUESTION 51: Staying in Touch with Customers

A question like this would make sense if you are involved with a sales or marketing function:

> **Q.** *I would like to know more about how you stay in touch with customers. What's the mix of courtesy calls, re-order calls, demonstrations and questionnaires that Yourco has found successful?*

It is important to remember that the customer is important to you in whatever function you have. An engineer might ask a question like this to show that she recognizes that fact:

> **Q.** *I am a skilled engineer, but I know that you don't want to make a product that doesn't have a market. How does the engineering staff get feedback and input from customers?*

Asking It Badly

It is important to respect everybody at Yourco no matter what their function. Would you hire someone who asked a question like this?:

Q. Does Yourco let creative people like me be productive, or do the bean counters and pencil geeks interfere with everything?

RE-ENGINEERING

Many firms today are being **re-engineered**. In principle that should mean a re-thinking of what needs to be done and how to do it. In practice, re-engineering may mean reducing a firm's work force and then determining how to get the same work load completed. In either case, there are a number of helpful questions you could ask.

QUESTION 52: Impact of Re-engineering

Q. *I read in the **Bellingham Bugle** that Yourco recently went through a re-engineering. About 50 people, 10% of the workforce were eliminated. Can you tell me if the results in terms of efficiency were about what you expected?*

You might wish to be a bit more pointed:

Q. *Yourco's recent re-engineering eliminated about 10% of the workforce. What has been the impact on manufacturing and customer service?*

or

Q. *After the recent re-engineering, how are the remaining employees dealing with their work load? Also, are people nervous about there being more cutbacks?*

QUESTION 53: Outsourcing

Sometimes a firm decides to buy some services or products from outside of the firm instead of producing them in house. A common term for this is outsourcing. There could be a professional impact on you even if your job isn't lost in the process.

> **Q.** *Many firms in the industry are outsourcing to produce greater efficiencies. When I read your annual report, I didn't notice any reference to this approach. Can you tell me what Yourco's plans for the future are in regard to outsourcing?*

or

> **Q.** *Yourco used to make its own paste for the Scissors and Paste product line. Now you are buying the paste from an outside vendor. Have there been any problems with product quality or reliability of service?*

or

> **Q.** *Yourco has been well known for a policy of promoting from within and growing its own talent. For reasons of competitive efficiency, the firm seems to be outsourcing more rather than relying on in-house staff. As the staff shrinks, will the potential for in house promotion shrink with it?*

Any of these questions show an interest in something which might affect you as it affects the firm. Each question also shows some prior research and thought. Compare the questions above with a **poor question** on the same topic:

Asking It Badly

Q. With all the re-engineering and outsourcing going on, would I still have a job a year from now?

Instead of asking a question which shows a professional, thoughtful approach, this question simply shows personal insecurity.

QUESTION 54: Strategic Alliances

Another common occurrence in today's business is forming strategic alliances. This might mean a pooling of resources, let's say for research. It could mean Myco will manufacture widgets and Yourco will sell them. Think about how a strategic alliance might impact on your function and then frame a question like this one:

Q. *Last year, Yourco formed a strategic alliance with Theirco to develop a new computer chip. I wonder if the respective finance and marketing functions are now talking to each other or if only the research area is operating differently.*

or

Q. *One of the things that has made Yourco so effective is the ability to make good decisions quickly. Is the alliance with Theirco going to slow decision making here?*

or

Q. *Sometimes when there is a strategic alliance, employees develop strong ties with their counterparts in the other company at the expense of in-house loyalties. Has that been a source of concern at Yourco?*

COMPANY PERFORMANCE

How's business? If business is great, people love to talk about it. When circumstances are more problematic, they need to be discussed frankly. Remember, an interview is a business meeting. You can prompt a discussion of company performance by asking at least one good question like those that follow:

QUESTION 55: Growth rate

> **Q.** *Yourco's annual report indicates that revenue has been growing at about 12% per year. Is that rate sustainable as the company grows larger?*

or

> **Q.** *. . . Is that rate going to accelerate due to the demographics of an aging America?*

or

> **Q.** *. . . Is the overall market large enough to sustain that growth rate, especially in light of increased competition?*

As with all questions:

- Make sure you **know** your facts; don't assume them.

- Be prepared for a response which includes a request for your own opinion.

QUESTION 56: Goals v. Performance

This question relates corporate goals to your prospective department:

> **Q.** *Yourco's Chairman, Mr. Greengrass, indicated that for the next three years cost cutting will be a major priority. Do you feel that this department will be budgeted enough resources to meet its performance goals?*

This question links goals with the decision making process:

Q. *I am interested in knowing how decisions about corporate goals are made. For example, Mr. Greengrass set the cost cutting goals for the next three years. Did the senior managers solicit input from the departments? Did they establish the goals and then you determined how to meet them?*

This question asks about not meeting goals:

Q. *At last year's stockholders meeting, there were many complaints about a relatively low earnings per share ratio. Did those stockholder concerns influence company goals or the way you do business?*

QUESTION 57: Benchmarking Through Competitors

It is true that firms compete in the marketplace. It is also true that firms may measure performance against publicly available information about competitors or other firms in general. Sometimes trade associations or conferences provide services for this information.

Q. *Setting realistic goals can be difficult. Does Yourco have any formal process for establishing goals by benchmarking against competitors' performance?*

or

Q. *Is senior management satisfied with this department's performance when benchmarked against competitors?*

or

Q. *You mentioned earlier that Yourco encourages employees to learn from the "best practices" of other firms. If the other firm is a competitor, what keeps best practices from being considered proprietary information?*

CORPORATE STRUCTURE AND RELATIONSHIPS

Remember that your questions should flow from knowledge and not ignorance. Basic research on the firm at which you will be interviewing should give you a good sense of how that firm is structured. Given what you know, you can ask some useful questions like these.

QUESTION 58: Business by Segments

> Q. *The annual report shows that the hand tool division has been more profitable than the power tool division for a number of years. Does the president of each division have authority to re-invest those profits on his/her own or is that a centralized decision of the corporation?*

or

> Q. *. . . Is that because they have had a better market or because of other factors?*

> Q. *. . . Do the two divisions do any joint marketing? Do they share any common resources?*

QUESTION 59: Relationship Among Functions

Remember that you will be part of a team striving to meet business goals. It is important that your loyalty to your own function (e.g. finance, information systems) doesn't interfere with the larger good. Let your interviewer know that you bring a cooperative approach to the job by asking a question like this.

> Q. *It takes a joint effort by different people to bring a product to market. Can you tell me what the relationship is among the finance, marketing and legal departments?*

or

> Q. *It seems that there are both vertical relationships within the division and horizontal relationships with the information systems people in the other divisions. Which relationships are the most important for this department?*

QUESTION 60: Melding of Cultures

There have been mergers, divestitures, and re-organizations throughout American business. The annual report will provide a sense of the formal relationships within a corporation. You may want to go beyond the organization chart and ask about the **informal** relationships or varying perspectives within the firm.

> **Q.** *Yourco has built its components division by buying several smaller firms. Have the combined staffs been able to meld their cultures?*

or

> **Q.** *As I understand it, decisions used to be made mostly in the corporate offices. Now it seems that the branches have been given more authority. How has the sharing of authority worked out? Are there any culture clashes between corporate and branch personnel?*

Asking It Badly

Q. Who is really in charge of things now?

FUTURE PLANS

It is a good idea to ask about the firm's plans for the future. After all, you hope to be a part of those plans. The next few questions let you express an interest in the future based on what you already know.

QUESTION 61: Using Technology

> **Q.** *I realize that there are restrictions about what you can tell me given the importance of protecting confidential proprietary information. Are you free to tell me if there are plans to upgrade the warehouse technology?*

or

Q. *I understand that the current accounting system uses software that's about three years old. Are any newer packages under consideration?*

or

Q. *Do you think that the Internet will offer any worthwhile advantages for Yourco's intra-corporate communication or research activities?*

QUESTION 62: Technological Change

The previous question dealt with the use of currently available technology. Yourco and your job may be affected at least as much by technologies still on the horizon. Many newspapers and news magazines now cover technology on a regular basis. You might want to ask a question like this one:

Q. *There is active discussion of creating a product which would play out the text of a book in a hand-held computer. Is Yourco Book Publishers considering ways to preserve the market for traditional books if such a new technology becomes popular?*

or

Q. *The automobile of the future may be self driving. You would simply program the vehicle with instructions. If such a thing comes to pass, should Yourco Hospitality Suites anticipate a larger long distance traveling market?*

Asking It Badly

Remember to show the relevance between the technology and Yourco or your job. Otherwise, you will give the impression that your head has been lost in cyberspace.

Q. I read a great article in *Technology Today* about a golf ball which can reach the green in a nanosecond. How will that impact on Yourco Antique Doll Company?

QUESTION 63: Plans for Globalization

Some firms are now viewing the entire world as their marketplace. This means that suppliers could be almost anywhere and so could customers. If your research shows that globalization is playing a significant role in Yourco you could ask:

Q. *I read in Widget Weekly that a full 25% of Yourco's sales were overseas last year, and key suppliers are now in Mexico and Brazil. But that was hardly the case as recently as ten years ago. How has this increasing involvement with foreign markets changed the way you manage the finance (or marketing or applications) function.*

or

Q. . . . *changed the way you conduct your daily business.*

or

Q. . . . *changed the skills you need to be successful at Yourco.*

Conversely, if Yourco is **not** involved in foreign markets, you could ask a question like this:

> Q. *I read in **Inc.** that Yourco's customer base is entirely domestic. Are there any plans to try foreign markets?*

QUESTION 64: American or Global Firm

One result of globalization can be a change in the corporation's perspective on itself.

> Q. *Yourco once publicized that its products were made in America and were a part of every American's family life. At that time the idea was "Made in America, Sold Around the World." Now suppliers, customers, even employees, come from around the world. In ten years will Yourco be an American company doing business internationally or a global company headquartered in America?*

This may seem like a long question, but the three sentences of prelude show you have done your research and puts the question in an intelligent perspective.

QUESTION 65: Foreign Ownership

Many businesses in the United States are owned by foreign based corporations. Japanese owned automobile companies are easy to identify, but British, Dutch, and Swiss owned enterprises are also quite common.

If you have followed Rule #2 (Read About; Thought About) you probably know if Yourco is foreign-owned. If it is, a question like this makes good sense.

> Q. *Does the fact that Yourco is Dutch owned make it easier to find markets for your products in Indonesia and other former Dutch colonies?*

or

> Q. *The international headquarters for Yourco is in London. Does the fact of British ownership effect the way you do business in the United States?*

or

Q. *Are the major decisions about research and marketing at Yourco made by American managers or by the Swedish owners in Stockholm?*

or

Q. *To what extent would we be concerned about foreign-exchange rates, given that Yourco's Swiss parent wants profits repatriated in Swiss currency?*

Asking It Badly

Q. How do Americans feel about having so many foreigners running this place?

QUESTION 66: Ownership Overseas

If Yourco is an American firm operating facilities overseas, that may also have a bearing on your job. You might want to ask a question like this one.

Q. *Yourco's annual report indicates that you own facilities in four different countries. Does the finance function in the United States have any direct contact with the managers overseas?*

or

Q. *Do Yourco's manufacturing plants overseas produce mostly for local markets or for export.*

or

Q. *Are the Yourco facilities overseas functionally connected with each other?*

or

Q. *Do the U.S. Managers at Yourco ever do a rotation in an overseas facility? If so, what skills do they need to succeed over there and what new skills do they bring back?*

QUESTION 67: Optimism

You can bring considerations of the future down to a more pragmatic level with a question like this:

Q. *Do you think employees are generally optimistic about the company's future and their future with the company?*

or

Q. *Do you sense that most people here are optimistic about Yourco returning to profitability next year?*

Asking It Badly

Q. I don't want to work for another company that's going to downsize. How secure would a job at Yourco be?

QUESTION 68: Company's Role as a Corporate Citizen

Some firms are very proud of the good causes they support. Perhaps the firm helps troubled youth, funds research or supports the arts. If the firm **is** a good corporate citizen, one upbeat question may be a good rapport builder.

Q. *I read in the local newspaper about your support for an after school tutoring program. How does Yourco determine what projects to support and do you encourage employer involvement?*

If you are not certain that the firm tries to be a good corporate citizen, don't raise the subject at your interview.

Asking It Badly

Be careful that you don't raise an appropriate subject in an inappropriate way.

Q. Are you guys going to do anything to improve your environmental record?

You might want to ask the question in terms of ethics.

Q. *The annual report reprinted Yourco's Code of Ethics. I thought it was very impressive. Are all employees made aware of the code?*

or

Q. *Have situations arisen in this department when the code was consulted for guidance?*

COMPANY AND WORKFORCE

QUESTION 69: Employees as Stakeholders

There are a number of reasonable questions you could ask about the workforce of your prospective new company. Here is a question with a philosophic bent:

Q. *There are different ways in which a company and its employees can relate. Some firms say they value their employees but treat them like labor inputs. Other firms consider employees to be stakeholders, on a par with stockholders. What is Yourco's approach?*

Hints: (1) Be prepared for a response which includes a question about employee relations on your current job or what your expectations are. (2) If the interviewer gives you a response that you find favorable, you could respond with a statement like "I am glad to hear that because I want to work for a firm that treats employees the way you do."

QUESTION 70: Labor Relations

Although unions are less prominent in American work life than a generation ago, they are still a significant factor in many industries. Irrespective of your personal philosophy, you could ask a question like the following:

Q. *Before coming in this morning, I asked the human resource department if Yourco has a unionized environment. They advised me that you do not. Do you see any discontent which might lead to a unionization drive in the future?*

or

Q. *Yourco hasn't experienced a strike for several years, but other firms in the industry have. How do you account for Yourco's apparently good labor relations?*

QUESTION 71: Entrepreneurial/Bureaucratic

You may want to ask a question about working environment which includes some insights about the future. For example:

Q. *We discussed Yourco's shirt-sleeves, first-name, open door approach to doing business. Do you think Yourco can avoid becoming more bureaucratic if it continues to grow at the present rate?*

or

Q. *Many firms find it difficult to retain an entrepreneurial management style as they have grown larger. What do you think will be the dominant operating style at Yourco in five years.*

QUESTION 72: Accessibility of CEO

No matter how entry level or senior your new position may be, you can ask about access to senior managers, like the CEO.

> **Q.** *How accessible is the CEO [name him or her if you can] to people at my level of the organization. Some firms have periodic meetings with employees, some have an open door policy, and some have a CEO who is a remote figure. How does it work at Yourco?*

Hints: (1) This question could be even better if you refer to something about the CEO you read in Yourco's annual report or in the press. (2) If you are happy with the response from the interviewer, say so. For example, "I am glad to hear that [the CEO] meets regularly with groups of employees. That's an attractive feature of working here". If you don't like the answer, proceed to your next question. (3) Here is an example of a question you could ask about a topic you discussed earlier in your interview.

> **Q.** *Earlier in our conversation you mentioned that Yourco's CEO is accessible to employees. Are there ground rules for approaching him (or her)?*

QUESTION 73: Staff Development

Let's say you are interviewing for a managerial position. Developing your employees is probably a major objective of your position. What resources are available to you to achieve your goal? Is your evaluation based on how much your staff produces, how rapidly they advance? Asking these question should indicate an interest in doing the job well in addition to providing you with some important information.

> **Q.** *Developing employees is mentioned in Yourco's annual report as a prime responsibility of managers. What kind of resources are available in addition to the manager's own skills? For example, is there a budget for conferences or in-house training?*

or

Q. *There are different ways firms develop staff. Some train today's staff to fit tomorrow's anticipated needs. Others weigh the employee's current interests and talents more heavily. What is the standard approach at Yourco?*

QUESTION 74: Bad News Questions

Sometimes your research reveals negative information about a company. For example, the firm may have lost money for several quarters, be fighting a serious lawsuit or be experiencing a major scandal. Should you ask about a company's bad news?

In general, the answer is "yes". Serious business people can face bad news. In fact, the firm may wish to openly discuss its problem as they understand it.

The key is to be tactful and ask your question in an appropriate manner.

Q. *People at Yourco must be talking about the disturbing news which was broadcast on Sunday's Fifty Minutes program. Do you sense that the story is causing any problems with suppliers?*

or

Q. *Most mutual funds in your category made a slim gain last year while your Fabulous Fifty portfolio took a substantial loss. Do you anticipate any major revisions in investment strategy?*

or

Q. *Yourco filed for bankruptcy last week. Do you feel that being protected from creditors gives this firm enough breathing room to get healthy again?*

Remember that an interview is a business meeting between equals. Your interviewer may ask potentially awkward questions **about you**. That is acceptable if the questions are asked in a non-offensive way. You may even welcome the opportunity to put a potentially unhelpful fact in a more favorable light. Your tactfully asked question gives your prospective employer the same opportunity.

The tone of your question is critical. Compare the **tactful** questions I gave you above with the **poorly** asked questions below:

Asking It Badly

Q. How does it feel to see your firm accused of fraud on a nationally broadcast television program.

Q. The market was up last year. How on earth did you manage to **lose** money?

Q. Why is a bankrupt company even bothering to interview people?

QUESTION 75: One Happy Family

Even in the happiest of families, there are tensions and arguments. This happens in corporate families also. Although you shouldn't dwell on it, one question about possible tensions in the firm would be appropriate.

Q. *The profits from this division at Yourco have been going to underwrite start-up costs for the Rainmaker division. How does management make sure that employees of this division don't feel like they are a colony for Rainmaker?*

or

Q. *Has the recent black eye that the service division got for overcharging hurt other divisions of the company?*

THE IMMEDIATE FUTURE

Many of the questions you could ask about the company are of a broad and sweeping nature. It is important to remember the issues which may affect your job in the very near future.

QUESTION 76: Next Year's Goals

Q. *The annual report discussed Yourco's goals over the long term. I would like to ask about some issues facing Yourco in the very near future. What are the top business priorities for the coming year and how will this department be involved in achieving them?*

or

Q. *. . . and how could I be helpful in achieving them?*

Q. *Yourco's annual report mentioned a four year plan to reduce costs by about 20%. How much of that goal is the firm trying to achieve in the next year?*

QUESTION 77: Your Involvement.

Q. *You mentioned earlier in the interview that this department will be introducing new audit controls next year. Can you tell me what prompted the changes? Also, I would like to know if I would be involved in implementing the new controls.*

YOURCO & CURRENT EVENTS

Staying current is part of your professional responsibilities in business. You can make a positive impression in your interview and gain valuable information for yourself by asking about current events involving your company. Since you have read about and thought about the company prior to your interview (remember Rule #2) you should be aware of what is being written about Yourco in either the general press or business publications.

Your question can be especially useful if it **relates** the news story to your particular job. Here are some examples to think about.

QUESTION 78: New Product

Q. *There have been several articles in the press about Yourco's new product, Flambang. Will the Marketing department try to position it as an upscale version of Flamping?*

or

Q. . . . *Will production and marketing of Flambang draw from employees in other parts of the company?*

or

Q. . . . *How could I help integrate Flambang into next year's budget?*

QUESTION 79: New CEO

You may read in the business section of your newspaper that Yourco will soon be getting a new CEO. Think about how this new CEO may affect Yourco and your potential job.

Q. *The news stories I read indicate that the incoming CEO, Suzanne Post, was selected because of her expertise in marketing. Do you think Yourco will shift from a manufacturing to a marketing emphasis now?*

or

Q. . . . *Do you think there will be some tension between Ms. Post and any of the current vice presidents who were passed over for the job?*

Asking It Badly

It is always possible to shoot yourself in the foot:

Q. Why on earth would Yourco hire someone from outside the firm? Isn't there any in-house talent?

or

Q. There aren't too many women CEO's. Was this just one of those affirmative action things?

QUESTION 80: Mission Statement

Many firms today have a mission statement which presents in broad terms the company's goals and operating philosophy. You can often find a company's mission statement in its annual report or acquire it through a simple phone call to Yourco's public relations department. A question about the firm's mission statement is appropriate irrespective of the position for which you are interviewing. However, try to relate it to your specific situation.

> **Q.** *Yourco's mission statement is very interesting. One part especially caught my attention. It discussed Yourco's commitment to quality service for clients, quality of work life for employees and due concern for stockholders' interests. In this position, should we consider all three commitments as having equal weight?*

or

> **Q.** *The mission statement made a point of stressing Yourco's belief in stewardship. In practice, situations may arise where what's best for Yourco in particular is not best for America in general. What guidelines does Yourco have for resolving conflicts between stewardship and profitability?*

In this chapter, we looked at forty (40) questions you could ask about the company. After doing the short exercises that follow, read the next chapter: Ten questions you could ask about the industry or profession.

Exercise 4

Part A contains a list of personal characteristics a person might have. Part B contains a number of questions a person might ask at his/her job interview. What characteristic is suggested by each question?

Part A

a. Confrontational   e. Me first personality

b. Interested in Pramatics of Firm   f. Keeps up with relevant
                                                business events
c. Has Researched Firm
                                            g. Revealing a weakness
d. Revealing Insecurity
                                            h. Has tact

Part B

1. It surprises me that Yourco doesn't sponsor sporting events the way Theirco does. How do you explain this oversight?

2. I have lots of bills to pay. How secure would this job be?

3. Competco is attracting younger clients by inviting people to MTV concerts. Is Yourco considering event sponsorship as a marketing tool?

4. Does this firm hold back the high flyers by letting the also-rans get in the way.

5. Business Week reported that Yourco's new Sleep For You service has struck a responsive chord with the overworked set who have no time to sleep for themselves. Do you think there is potential for a spin-off service for people who don't have time to eat their own food?

6. I don't have the patience for staff who just don't understand what I want. What's the process for eliminating folks like that?

7. As you know, there was a report in the newspaper that Yourco has been accused of stealing the patent rights to Fizzo. Is this issue causing any concern at Yourco?

8. Yourco has recently organized projects around teams from

different functions. How has the transition to this approach been received by employees?

Our Answers			
1. a	2. d	3. c	4. e
5. c	6. g	7. h	8. b

Exercise 5

Read the following section from Yourco's annual report. Then write at least three questions you could ask based on what you have read:

"The past year has produced mixed results for Yourco. While our Gadgetco division recorded a record 236% increase in profits, the Widget division is in its third straight year of losses.

Management is committed to both divisions. We are confident that the re-engineering process in place at both divisions will produce a stronger Yourco to meet the challenge of both domestic and foreign competition in the years ahead. We will not sacrifice market share to obtain these goals."

Helpful Hint: These samples from Chapter 4 should help you write your own questions: Questions #41, 44, 48, 52, 56, 58, 66, 72, 74.

For example, you could ask a question like this:

Q. *The annual report mentioned that the Gadgetco division showed record profits last year while the Widget division experienced its third year of losses. Has there been any sharing of staff resources between the divisions to help Widgetco return to profitability?*

or

Q. *Is the re-engineering process at Yourco similar or different for the two divisions?*

Exercise 6

The following news story about Yourco appears in the *Daily Bugle:*

> Yourco announced today that it is planning several significant
> moves over the next two years. The nation's second largest gadget
> maker will build a new factory in Factorville for its Series C
> mouse trap. This is about 200 miles from the current site adjacent
> to Yourco headquarters. Sales offices will be opened in the
> regional centers instead of relying on the central marketing staff.
> "If we are to remain an industry leader, we need to re-think about
> ways to retain an entrepreneurial spirit and best use our resources,"
> Julian Smith, an SVP told a crowded news conference.

Helpful Hint: We found the following questions from Chapter 4 could
flow from this newspaper item: Questions 42, 48, 59, 69, 71, 76.
For example:

Q. *The Daily Bugle reported that Yourco is committed to getting
the most from its human resources while relocating some of
the manufacturing and sales functions. What resources would
I have as a manager to help my staff adjust to the new
situation and become even more productive?*

5

THE INDUSTRY OR PROFESSION: TEN QUESTIONS YOU COULD ASK

KEEP YOUR GOAL IN MIND

Most successful people keep current with happenings throughout their industry, not just their particular firm. There is a good reason for this: business doesn't exist in a vacuum. Knowing about trends in the industry, how other firms adjust to new situations, and how your firm measures up to the industry standard is necessary for success. I suggest that you ask one question about the industry; more if you have already asked several questions about the job and the firm.

Sometimes it is more appropriate to think in terms of profession, rather than industry. Public accounting and health care would be examples.

QUESTION 81: Export Orientation

Q. *Standard & Poor's Industry Surveys reported that the industry as a whole is becoming more export oriented. Do you think that trend can be sustained in light of competition from low wage but technologically competent countries.*

This question shows that you have done some research and are thinking about potential challenges that confront decision makers throughout the industry.

Caution: Make sure you know your facts. In this case, be certain that there really could be competition from other countries for your potential employer's markets. **Don't assume** that a fact which is broadly applicable applies in your specific situation.

A related question could be this:

Q. *The relative strength or weakness of the American dollar is a factor in exports. Do you think that trade groups in this industry are adequately concerned about this?*

QUESTION 82: Trade Treaties

It is important to be current with news and anticipate possible implications for your industry. The following question gives an example, regarding imports.

Q. *Many of the critical components utilized in this industry are produced overseas. How have GATT & NAFTA affected sourcing strategies?*

Hint: Be prepared for a response which includes: "I wonder if **you** have any ideas about how to take advantage of reduced or eliminated tariffs." If you followed the first two rules for asking a question (you really care; you have read about and thought about the issue) you **should have** some ideas of your own.

You might want to ask about an anticipated or potential trade agreement:

Q. *If Japan agrees to be more accommodating to imports, will Yourco try to find a market there?*

or

Q. *There is a possibility that the U.S. will impose a high tariff on Japanese-made imports. Since Yourco imports components from Japan, are you looking for alternative sources?*

QUESTION 83: Size of Firms

There may be some industry wide trends which could affect your particular job. This example assumes you are in product development, but it could be structured to apply to different jobs as well.

Q. *Industry Monthly predicted that there will be a consolidation of firms within this industry resulting in fewer but larger firms. Do you think that consolidation would put new product development on hold or would it lead to increased availability of resources?*

This question may be difficult to answer with certainty. After all, consolidations if they occur, could happen in different combinations and with different strategic goals. That's all right. Sometimes the value of a question lies in prompting serious thought. Besides, this question shows the ability to relate an industry-wide event to your particular job. That says something good about you. In addition, the question is about something you should want to know.

Asking It Badly

Q. Largeco just bought Mediumco. What does that mean for Yourco?

or

Q. Yourco is number three in the industry. Do firms of this size have a future?

The problem with these two questions is this: Although each question indicates knowledge of a fact, neither question indicates that you have given the fact any thought.

QUESTION 84: Integrated Companies or Virtual Corporations

In your industry, size **per se** may not be the operative question. Instead, there may be a trend towards integrating most functions within one company instead of relying on outside vendors. There is also an opposite trend toward virtual corporations. A simple way of thinking of a virtual corporation is that most functions are carried out by outside contractors with whom specific commitments of limited duration have been made. Will you be working with fellow employees from different functions or with a changing cast of outside vendors?

Q. *We all have to be prepared for changes in the way firms do business. I notice from reading* **Business Monthly** *that some firms in the industry have decided to integrate their functions while some others are moving towards being virtual corporations. Which trend do you think will dominate over the next five years?*

or

Q. *As you look over the firms in this industry, some have retained a traditional structure, some have become more integrated and* *still others have become virtual corporations. Is Yourco evaluating the advantages of each approach?*

Caveat: Remember Rule #5: Make sure you are asking a person who might reasonably be expected to be familiar with this issue.

or

Q. *A number of leading firms in this industry have decided to bring more functions in house. Sales and service are examples. Do you think that similar changes will impact manufacturing processes as well?*

QUESTION 85: Mergers/Restructuring

Are firms in your industry going to get larger or smaller? Commercial banks are merging to aggregate financial resources and cut administrative expenses. Some consumer product firms are cutting levels of staff, in part to make decision making faster. Your work life, and even your job itself, may depend on how firms in your industry view the issue of ideal size.

Q. *The business press carries stories about companies getting larger through acquisitions and other firms slimming down through re-engineering and outsourcing. Several firms in this industry have merged in the last year. Do you think this will establish an industry trend? If it does, will Yourco also seek merger partners?*

It is possible to ask a question badly even when you have a good topic.

Asking It Badly

Q. Do you think mergers will result in more layoffs in this industry?

Asked this way, the question shows insecurity rather than insight.

QUESTION 86: Impact of Interest Rates

Some industries, like housing and automobiles, are very sensitive to interest rates. People generally borrow to purchase a home or car, so interest rates influence the size of monthly payments. You may want to ask about interest rates even if your function does not deal directly with them.

Q. *The automobile industry is sensitive to interest rates. Does this firm try to plan according to anticipated rates or does it make adjustments based on actual rates?*

or

Q. *When we consider the optimum pricing for our product, to what extent do we factor-in a range of potential interest rates?*

or

Q. *When Yourco plans the number of windshields to manufacture, does it use orders in hand or does it estimate windshield demand as a function of anticipated auto sales?*

Asking It Badly

Q. Do interest rates have any impact on this industry?

Stated this way, the question vilolates Rule #2 (Read about; Thought about) and probably Rule #1 (Care about) and Rule #4 (Barrier Free) as well.

QUESTION 87: The Players, How Many and How Strong?

What will the cast of leading players in Yourco's industry look like in the future?

Q. *This is a tough industry to succeed in. Right now each of the four main players is dominant in a particular area of the country. Do you think somebody is going to try to become dominant nationally? Will Yourco?*

or

Q. *There are three main players in this industry. How many do you think there will be in ten years?*

or

Q. *Do you think it is possible for a new player to become significant in this industry by developing a dramatically new or improved product?*

Asking It Badly

Q. Who is going to be Number 1 in a few years?

QUESTION 88: Powers of Scale

There are various ways that firms in an industry can try to cut costs. In a manufacturing environment, there is potential for economies of scale. For example, it is possible to reduce the unit cost of making widgets by spreading fixed production costs over more widgets.

In a merchandising environment, a large distributor is such a critical customer that it can strike a favorable deal with suppliers.

You might want to ask a question like this one.

Q. *Tough negotiating with suppliers is one way to cut costs. Do the firms in this industry have enough clout to buy at favorable prices?*

or

Q. *Do you think that Yourco or other firms in the industry will aggressively seek to get more orders to take advantage of economies of scale?*

or

Q. *Do you think that Yourco will seek a merger within the industry to strengthen its competitive position through economies of scale?*

QUESTION 89: Government Regulation and Legislation (Industry Stance)

Earlier, we suggested a question about government regulation and the firm with which you are interviewing. You could ask this question in addition, perhaps as a follow-up.

Q. *On the surface of it, every firm in this industry has to live with government regulation. Is there a common industry approach to the government or does each firm try to bend regulations to their own advantage?*

or

Q. *One of the serious tax proposals in Congress is to replace the income tax, including corporate, to a VAT (Value Added Tax). How would a VAT effect Yourco and is there any industry stance on the subject?*

QUESTION 90: Industry Partners

In some industries, firms have formed alliances to develop a new product or to provide a service jointly. Is that approach possible in Yourco's industry?

Q. *It seems that client demands may overwhelm any given firm in this industry. Do you think some of the firm's may form alliances so that each can provide part of the overall service to the same client?*

or

Q. *In some industries, firms have formed partnerships on specific issues, even with competitors. Given Yourco's desire to do more Research & Development, do you think such a partnership is possible, perhaps for widget safety and new widget uses?*

or

Q. *There is considerable political interest in public/ private partnerships, especially in states where privatization of government functions is an issue. Do you see any potential for such partnerships in this industry?*

This chapter gave you examples of questions to ask about your prospective firm's industry. In the next chapter we will look at questions about external influences.

Exercise 7

This exercise is designed to help you experience the message your questions might send to your interviewer. In Part A, you will find a list of personal characteristics. Part B contains questions a person might ask at his/her interview. What characteristic is suggested by each question?

Part A

a. Me First
b. Can think at a managerial level
c. Poor listening skills
d. Research industry

e. Thinks about what s/he hears
f. Insecurity
g. Can relate general to the specific
h. Reveals a weakness

1. Is this industry going to be destroyed by foreign competition the way hand tools was?

2. *Business Week* reported that widgets may soon become more like a standardized commodity than a specialized tool. If that prediction comes true, how will Yourco continue to position itself as the premier widget maker in the industry?

3. Are salaries in this industry competitive with other industries?

4. *Industry Monthly* reported that firms in this industry are losing good staff to the Gadget Industry because there seem to be more lucrative opportunities there. Do you think this trend can be reversed?

5. I am not a very technical person. Is that a disadvantage in this industry?

6. When you think about your counterparts in other firms in this industry, are there any skills or characteristics they seem to have in common?

7. This industry seems complicated but interesting. Can you repeat what you told me about it?

8. You mentioned earlier that this industry has tended to change slowly in the past. Do you think innovation will be more rapid now that foreign competition is becoming a major factor?

Our Answers

1. f	5. h
2. g	6. b
3. a	7. c; also probably didn't do much research
4. d	8. e

Exercise 8

Suppose you read this in Yourco's annual report:

"As the domestic market has matured, Yourco has increasingly sought more export opportunities. We believe that trade with

Mexico and Asia will be especially important. Our greatest challenges will be intense competition, both domestic and foreign, and excessive government regulation which has hobbled our industry."

What questions about the industry could you ask based on the text above?

Helpful Hint

These questions from Chapter 5 relate to the quotation from Yourco's annual report: Questions 81, 82, 89.

6

EXTERNAL INFLUENCES: 10 QUESTIONS YOU COULD ASK

KEEP YOUR GOAL IN MIND

One purpose of your questions is to show that you can think professionally along a whole spectrum of issues. Your questions about external influences should identify factors which could impact your job, company or industry even though they are separate from them. Government regulation, political events and international news offer some examples. These questions should show you are thinking about external events which may touch very close to your professional life.

People who can think this way are highly promotable and therefore more desirable to hire in the first place.

In addition, it is a good idea to find out more about how the industry, Yourco and your new job relate to each other.

As with all questions, remember to follow the Five Rules we discussed in Chapter 2.

- You care.
- You have read about and thought about the issue.
- The answer is not in some obvious place.
- The question doesn't raise a barrier to hiring you.
- The question is appropriate for the interviewer.

QUESTION 91: Foreign Currency Changes

Q. *Given the instability of currency exchange rates, how is this firm protecting itself from problems like the steep depreciation of the Mexican peso in 1995?*

If your function deals with exports to Mexico or manufacturing there, you would have an interest in Mexico's political and economic stability. However, don't ask the question just to show that you know something about the peso. Every question should have a bearing on your objectives for this meeting—i.e. to convince the firm to offer you the job you want or to gain information you may need to know.

In a similar vein, make sure you are raising the issue intelligently. If the firm does all its trade with Denmark, a question about the krona makes sense. A question about the peso does not.

Make sure that the firm's annual report or the front page of *Business Week* do not provide the answer to your question. A readily available item of information should be a source of questions, not a source of embarrassment.

QUESTION 92: Consumer Taste

Another largely external influence is changes in consumer taste. Anticipating change, or at least keeping up with it, is a necessity to survive in today's business. Show that you can link a changing situation to your firm's business with a question like this:

Q. *Consumers seem to be increasingly health conscious. Yourco's products have sold based on great taste. Are you free to share with me any plans to modify or add products that appeal to the more health conscious consumer?*

Hint: As always, listen carefully to the interviewer's response. Perhaps it will provide an opening for you. For example, "I am glad to hear that you are exploring a high protein, low calorie chocolate mousse. At Tastyco, I worked on a project to produce a packaged ice cream sandwich which was outside our usual product line. It was difficult to position Handy-Yum correctly, but it has been very profitable."

Another way you could ask about consumer taste is this:

Q. *When times are prosperous, consumers of products like Yourco's seem to put a premium on a high quality, deluxe product. In recessionary times, price seems to be much more important. To what extent does Yourco try to anticipate economic trends when planning its product mix?*

or

Q. *I read in the San Francisco Chronicle that high yields seem to be gaining importance over caution when people choose mutual funds. Do you think that Yourco Financial Services should develop more high yield, high risk funds?*

QUESTION 93: Technological Change

Another kind of change is brought about by technology. A thoughtful question about the impact of technological change on your company or job can help present you in a positive light and provide you with important information.

Q. *Technological change is a fact of life. How is Yourco utilizing the Internet to access sources of consumer information?*

or

Q. *With bar codes, scanners and up-to-date computers, it is possible for huge supermarkets to keep a reasonably good check on inventory. Do you think it will be possible and beneficial to apply similar technology to goods in process at Yourco's Manufacturing division?*

or

Q. *One of the things you mentioned earlier is that Yourco keeps most administrators in one building to facilitate face-to-face communication. Will teleconferencing and picture screen telephones lead to a greater geographical dispersion of the staff?*

or

Q. *I read in **Aircraft Monthly** that new technology is making it possible to build engines which are far more fuel efficient. Do you think our clients would be willing to pay a greater initial cost for fuel efficiency when the price of aviation may not be a big factor in future years?*

QUESTION 94: Trade Treaties and Tariff Status

International trade treaties and bi-lateral trade negotiations can significantly impact on what can be bought and at what price. Consumers are affected and so is every firm which utilizes, sells or competes with the imported products. A person who reads a good daily newspaper should be able to ask a knowledgeable question like this one:

Q. *Yourco has been successful in developing a market for a superior product at a moderately higher price. Chinese built products can be of excellent quality but production costs are lower. If China retains the privilege of low tariffs through its MFN (Most Favored Nation) status, will they be undercutting Yourco's domestic market?*

or

Q. *The Administration seems to be trying to gain freer access for American products in the Japanese markets. Do you foresee any solid opportunities for Yourco in Japan?*

or

Q. *The Law of the Sea Convention may become international law at some point. Yourco utilizes some of the natural resources which can be found in the sea bed. Will the sea become a source of raw materials for Yourco?*

THE IMPACT OF GOVERNMENT

QUESTION 95: Impact of (De) Regulation

Whatever our political sympathies, we know that government policy influences the economy. Some industries are directly regulated (e.g. investment securities through the SEC), some less directly regulated (e.g. consumer product safety through the FTC) and some are influenced by legislation (e.g. cars through domestic content laws.)

Since government regulation and legislation are public policy issues, both the trade publications and the general press carry discussion about them. You have two tasks in formulating a question.

- Know the issues
- Apply them to your industry, company and/or job

Your question might sound like this:

Q. *There is some talk in Congress of loosening consumer product safety regulation. While regulation can be a burden, it can also increase consumer confidence in our products. On balance, how has consumer product safety legislation impacted on Yourco?*

or

Q. *Benefits Monthly had a recent article about firms shifting to a 401(K) approach rather than a company pension, in part because of government regulation. As a human resource professional, I know that employees are very concerned about pensions just as firms are concerned about controlling cost. Is Yourco considering a shift to the 401(K) system?*

Hint: Don't just ask "how has government regulation impacted on this firm?" Remember rule #2. Your question
should show that you have **read** about and **thought**
about the issue.

QUESTION 96: Dependence on Government

An alternate question could reflect the fact that some products owe their
existence to government regulation, actual or anticipated. For example,
the electric car depends on those state governments which insist that
some percentage of automobiles sold be pollution free. Some insurance
policies are designed to minimize inheritance taxes and avoid probate.
Municiple bonds are popular because they are tax exempt. To what
extent is your potential employer's product dependent on government
policy?

> **Q.** *Yourco's second best selling product is the MowerGuard
> which it sells to lawn mower manufacturers. This device
> prevents lawn mowers from cutting people instead of grass.
> Although it is expensive, it is being sold to manufacturers as
> a safeguard against product liability suits. If the federal
> government restricts awards in product liability cases, will
> MowerGuard lose its market?*

or

> **Q.** *Earlier you mentioned that a large percentage of the residents
> at Yourco Nursing Home, Inc. receive assistance through
> Medicare or Medicaid. Both programs may undergo serious
> cutbacks. Can you tell me what plans Yourco may have to deal
> with this eventuality?*

QUESTION 97: Federal Budget & Deficit

All levels of government can influence the environment of business, but
let's limit this sample question to the federal government. The federal
budget can influence your work situation in at least two ways:

- How the money is spent
- The size of the deficit

Let's say that you want to work in agribusiness or the supermarket industry or product packaging. All are influenced by the Food Stamp Program because it enables low income individuals to buy products they otherwise could not. Food Stamps, designed for the poor, also increase demand for businesses involved with food. Thus even a person making a good income might ask a question like this:

> **Q.** *Food Industry News reported that over 25 million U.S. residents utilize food stamps. Does this firm adjust product size, selection or price to reflect purchasing patterns in low income areas?*

The federal government deficit could also affect Yourco.

> **Q.** *There seems to be a consensus that the federal deficit should be reduced, although there is political disagreement over ways to do it. With the deficit shrinking, has it become easier to borrow capital funds Yourco needs for expansion?*

QUESTION 98: Popular Pressure

Consumer taste and government policy can both impact on business. Popular pressure is an external factor because it might shift consumer taste or influence government policy. Environmental concerns are one example.

Many environmentally conscious citizens have been concerned about packaging. For example, a large container of detergent uses more plastic and takes up more space in the town dump than a small one. Responding to concerns of this kind, detergent manufacturers have developed high power, concentrated product yielding more cleaning power in a smaller bottle. Think about how environmental concerns might affect you professionally. Your question could be like this one:

> **Q.** *Many people are very concerned about conserving natural resources. Will there be more emphasis on building Yourco's product from recyclable materials?*

or

> **Q.** *Wide-spread concern about the ozone layer has led to new regulations which have dramatically increased the cost of*

Freon. Are Yourco's airconditioners harder to sell because they are more expensive or easier to sell because they are environmentally more friendly?

QUESTION 99: International News

Events thousands of miles from Yourco can have an enormous impact on its business. Sometimes the impact is clear and direct, but sometimes what's good for the world may not be good for Yourco. Think about events reported in the daily newspaper and relate it to Yourco or your job.

Q. *Yourco's best selling car is so popular because it gets 40 miles per gallon on the highway. However, if Russia can stabilize, it may be able to export more oil than it currently does. Peace in the Middle East may soon become a reality. If this good news for peace lowers the price of oil, will there still be a healthy market for fuel efficient automobiles like Yourco's?*

or

Q. *The profitability of Yourco's airplane engines is really in the service and parts contract. Yourco's biggest client in recent years has been China. Are Yourco's contracts at risk when China's elderly leadership passes from the scene?*

QUESTION 100: The Worst Nightmare

Any number of events beyond a firm's control can influence its business. Unanticipated concerns about asbestos affects builders and insurers. Plane crashes hurt airlines as well as kill passengers. You could ask a general question about external events which might concern the firm or industry.

Q. *Asbestos dangers rocked builders and insurance companies, public attitudes are affecting tobacco companies. What are some potential dangers which would harm this industry or firm?*

A more specific question would be better:

Q. *From what I read in the business press, CD-ROM's may make the traditional encyclopedia and conventional trade books obsolete. Does Yourco Publishing see this as a serious threat to the industry?*

or

Q. *Independent commercial fishing boats are having a hard time making ends meet. Will Yourco Cannery be able to operate profitably if we have to buy fish only from the large fleet owners?*

In this chapter we looked at ten sample questions you could ask about external influences on Yourco or on its industry. Before starting the next chapter, work on Exercises 9 and 10

In Chapter 7, we will look at asking for the job—and deciding whether to accept it.

Exercise 9

Assume that you read the following article in the newspaper.

"Trade Tensions between the United States and Japan are causing reverberations beyond the products currently being subjected to tariffs and other restrictions. For example, fluctuations in currency exchange rates are causing uncertainty about pricing policy for a widgets & gadgets, although these items are not directly imported into the United States. Further, the viability of the recently born WTO (World Trade Organization) seems to be in doubt. Some fear that popular pressure in both Japan and the United States will limit the options for a compromise settlement. 'A full scale trade war would be the worst scenario we can imagine,' said Seth Richards, president of the Discretionary Income Products Association."

Write three questions about external events based on this newspaper article:

A Broad Hint

As we read this quotation, these questions from Chapter 6 came to mind: Questions 91, 94, 98, 99, 100.

Exercise 10

Will your questions help you get the job offer? It depends on what you ask and how you ask it. Read the questions below. Will they help or hurt the job candidate.

1. I read in the *San Francisco Chronicle* that Chile imported 10,000 cars from Japan last year. What does that mean for Yourco?

2. The new government in France is committed to reducing unemployment there. Is there any sign that France will impose barriers to Yourco's exports to France?

3. Consumer taste is so fickle, don't you think?

4. In your experience, how has Yourco been able to anticipate shifts in consumer taste in enough time to adjust product mix decisions effectively.

5. Many of Yourco's best customers for the vacation division are senior citizens. If the Medicare Program covers less of their medical expenses in the future, the older folks may cut back on vacations in order to pay their medical bills. Is Yourco considering a strategy to address that eventuality?

6. How has government policy affected Yourco?

Our View

In our view, this is how the questions in Exercise 10 would effect the prospects of the candidate who asks them.

1. **It depends.** This question could be helpful if Yourco exports cars to Chile. In that case it would have been better to ask "...will the Japanese imports hurt Yourco's market in Chile". As the question is stated in the exercise, however, it would hurt the candidate if there is no identifiable connection between the Japanese cars in Chile and Yourco.

2. **Probably helpful.** It shows that the job candidate can relate a foreign political development to Yourco's situation.

3. **Probably hurts.** The question should flow from sincere intent and what the applicant has read about and thought about. Neither seems to be the case here.

4. **Probably helps.** Because it links the external situation to Yourco's particular case.

5. **Almost certainly helpful.** This question shows that the job applicant can identify an issue that has a profound, but indirect impact on Yourco.

6. **Probably hurts.** This question shows no prior research or thought.

7

CLOSING: THE ONE QUESTION YOU SHOULD ALWAYS ASK

QUESTION 101: "Next Step" and How to Ask For the Job.

What's wrong with this picture? You have worked hard to build and present an impressive resume. You have succeeded in arranging an interview for the job of your dreams. You prepared well. Your answers are terrific and your questions are even better. Your interviewer says, "John, it has been a pleasure meeting you. We will be in touch with you soon." You respond, "Thank you, it has been a pleasure meeting you and I hope to hear from you soon."

Something is missing. You have just been to a business meeting. It is important to **close for something.** Ask for the job! There are several ways to do this. Pick the approach which best fits your personality.

Q. *It has been a pleasure meeting with you, too, Carol. Based on what we discussed today, do you anticipate offering me the position?*

or

Q. *It has been a pleasure meeting you, too, Carol. I really want this job. Can you tell me what our next step will be?*

In all likelihood, you will get a thoroughly non-committal response like "We have a number of candidates to interview. You should be hearing from us in about two weeks." Don't worry, the point of asking for the job **is not** to get an immediate, definitive response. Your goal is to nudge the ultimate response in your favor. There are at least **five** reasons why asking for the job will help you get it:

- **Good Business Practice:** Business meetings, including interviews, should end with some sense of what has been accomplished. By asking for the job, you have demonstrated an appropriate sense of purpose.

- **Assuring the Interviewer:** It is difficult to ask for something unless you really want it. Your closing statement should allay concerns the interviewer may have about your degree of interest in the job.

- **Better Preparation:** If you know that you are going to ask for the job at the end of the interview, you will have an added incentive to prepare well before hand.

- **It's easier for someone to like you** if you say "I like you" first. It gives the other person a sense of security. Then it is easier for them to say "I like you, too," e.g. to invite you to a follow-up interview or even offer you the job.

- **Gumption:** An appropriate degree of gumption is a positive characteristic. Show you have gumption by asking for the job.

> In the unlikely event that the job is offered to you on the spot, you can say "That's really terrific. I am really excited about a job offer from Yourco. When do you need to have my response?"

SALES INTERVIEW

A special note: If you are interviewing for a sales position, asking for the job is more than helpful—it is critical. If you don't ask for the job, you probably won't get it. After all, the job of a sales representative is to close the deal, not just make a nice presentation. Phrases like these would be useful.

- "I really want this job. Am I going to get it?"
- "Did I get the job?"
- "I want this job. When can we meet for a follow-up interview?"

QUESTIONS TO ASK YOURSELF

We have stressed throughout this book that your interview questions have two purposes: (1) to help you get the job offer by showing that you have the needed qualities; (2) to help you understand better what your new work situation would be like.

The first purpose is over when you go down the elevator at interview's end. The second purpose, learning from the interviewer's responses, now becomes paramount.

Review each question you asked and think about:

- **How did the interviewer react?** Was the interviewer comfortable responding to your question?

- **What did you learn** from the substance of the response? If you have a follow-up interview, do you want to pursue the issue? If you get the job offer, interviewers' responses should weigh in your decision.

- **Were you comfortable** asking the question? If not, was it because you were concerned about the interviewer's reaction? You should remember that an interview is a business meeting between equals. Beyond that, warning bells should go off in your mind. Does the interviewer's discomfort suggest a reason for not accepting the job if offered? Was it because the question didn't meet the Five Rules (see Chapter 2)? In that case, think about the question.

This self review will help you if you pursue this job opportunity further and also if you interview with another firm.

THE JOB OFFER

Here's another picture to contemplate:

It is some days after your hiring interview at Yourco. The phone starts to ring. It's Rhonda, the hiring manager for the position at Yourco. Your heart pounds but you retain your composure as Rhonda offers you the job you prepared so hard to get. Now what?

The **first** thing you want to do is thank Rhonda for the offer, telling her how excited you are. The **second** thing you should do is ask Rhonda, "When do you need to hear from me?", namely her decision date or deadline for a response. **Third** you want to ask Rhonda when you should expect to receive a **written** copy of the offer.

The last thing you want to do is give Rhonda an immediate response. Here's why:

- You don't want to make a major decision in the **flush of excitement.**

- You need to carefully **weigh the job offer** against your own set of criteria.

- You may be able to **negotiate for better terms**, assuming the job itself is of interest to you.

Let's look at each of these three reasons individually.

FLUSH OF EXCITEMENT

You probably worked hard to earn this job offer. What's more, the job search process often puts your ego on the line. If you are pressed by circumstance to find a new job, your emotions are involved all the more. So when you get the job offer you are excited, perhaps also vindicated and relieved.

Calm down and think through your options very carefully. Accepting a job offer is a major decision. You don't want to wake up one morning and regret that your excitement precluded a sober judgement.

WEIGHING YOUR JOB OFFER

You applied for the position and interviewed in good faith, namely you had a serious interest in the job. But you are not morally obligated to **accept** this job. You have other options to consider, including keeping your current job, accepting another offer or pursuing your job search until you land a better offer.

It is important to both Yourco and you that you go into a new job with your eyes open and with enthusiasm. Therefore once the job offer has been obtained you should evaluate it very carefully. The following four step evaluation should help you make your decision.

STEP 1:   Full list of what you want

STEP 2:   How important is each criterion

STEP 3:   How well does Yourco's offer satisfy each criterion

STEP 4:   Overall evaluation

Your list of criteria and degree of satisfaction will probably differ from those presented in the chart on page 105, but this sample gives you the idea.

Looking at this chart, you would see that the job Yourco offers seems to meet your expectation in terms of challenge/interest. You would prefer greater promotional potential but your assessment is that it's still good. The commute could be shorter, but that seems to be a marginal concern over a low priority issue. It seems that your comfort with the corporate culture belongs in the wait and see category. The one area where Yourco could realistically improve its offer is compensation.

Once you have concluded that you want the job **except a small number of reservations** (hopefully no more than one), you are in a position to negotiate the terms of your offer.

(1)	(2)	(3)	(4)	(5)	(6)
My Criteria	Realistic Expectations	How Important is it? (Based on 100 pts)	Yourco's Offer	Offer Compared to Goal	How Happy (Col3 x Col5)
Compensation	$50,000	25	$40,000	.80	20
Commute	40 Minutes	15	60 Minutes	.66	10
Challenge/ Interest	Very	25	Very	1.00	25
Promotional Potential	High	20	Moderate	.75	15
Comfort w/ Corporate Culture	I'm Flexible	15	Unsure	.67	10

NEGOTIATING YOUR OFFER

You are in the strongest bargaining position if you sincerely want the job **but** you are hesitating to say "yes" for a reason that the firm could plausibly address. Compensation is an obvious example; starting date, job title, salary review date, support services are others. Negotiating for better terms is part of business, but Yourco will be reluctant to offer you more if you might say "no" anyway. Therefore you should say to the person who extended you the offer:

"Rhonda, I am excited about this job. I like what I would be doing, the people I would be working with and I like Yourco overall. I am hesitating to say "yes", though, because of the compensation. I was expecting an offer in the low $50's. If you could increase the compensation towards that expectation, I would say "yes" right away."

Notice that you don't say, "I will only accept if ..." or "I won't accept unless ...". Be careful to leave room for agreement if Yourco's revised offer is still less than you expected.

ACCEPTING/REJECTING

If you do decide to accept Yourco's offer, speak to Rhonda and tell her so. Then follow-up with a written acceptance. Your letter could look like this one:

Acceptance Letter

2123 Caldwell Street
Havertown, PA 19053

November 11, 1995

Ms. Rhonda Goodman
Vice President, Marketing
Yourco
1515 Walnut Street
Philadelphia, PA 19104

Dear Rhonda,

It was wonderful speaking with you again on November 9. As you and I discussed then, I am delighted with Yourco's revised offer contained in your letter of November 8 and I am pleased to accept it.

To review the substance of our agreement, I will join your staff in Philadelphia on December 1. My title will be Manager of Marketing Promotions, with an annual salary of $48,000 plus benefits.

I look forward to joining Yourco and making a solid contribution from day one.

Sincerely,

Lauren Richardson

Of course, it is possible that you will reject Yourco's offer. Rejections, like acceptances, should be conveyed orally and in writing. Your letter **rejecting** Yourco's offer might look like this:

Rejection Letter

2123 Caldwell Street
Havertown, PA 19053

November 11, 1995

Ms. Rhonda Goodman
Vice President, Marketing
Yourco
1515 Walnut Street
Philadelphia, PA 19104

Dear Rhonda,

It was wonderful speaking with you again on November 9. As you and I discussed, I must reluctantly decline your offer of employment with Yourco. The job truly excited me and I looked forward to joining your staff. Unfortunately we couldn't agree on mutually acceptable terms.

I am pleased that we had the chance to meet. Perhaps we will run into each other at a future meeting of the Madcap Marketing Association.

On a personal matter, please maintain the confidentiality of our discussions as I am remaining with my current employer.

Sincerely,

Lauren Richardson

In this chapter, we looked at the one question that you should **always** ask your interviewers and some questions to ask yourself, including "Do I Want To Accept This Job Offer?" In the next chapter, we take a look at some sources you can use when researching material for your questions.

8

QUICK RESEARCH TO GIVE YOUR QUESTIONS THE GREATEST IMPACT

Throughout the 101 questions presented here, we have usually referred to some research which preceded the question. You may have wondered about two things:

- finding the sources;
- finding the time to read them.

Let's look at both these issues.

FINDING THE SOURCES

You may already be conversant with the general issues which affect your job, company or industry. If you are, it is important that you go beyond conversance and build a degree of expertise. Further you want to show the application of your understanding to the situation of your next employer.

If you are a stranger to the issues which are important to your next employer, you have some extra work to do.

In either case, let's take a look at some easy method to find sources which can provide a wealth of information.

ANNUAL REPORT

If an American company is publicly held (i.e. it sells shares of common stock to the public), it must issue an annual report. You can acquire one easily by calling the firm's corporate headquarters, contacting a stock broker or visiting a good library. For your interview questions, these are the most important parts of an annual report.

- **Message to Shareholders:** Usually written by the Chairman, President or CEO, this message provides several pages of information. Typically there is a page or so reviewing the previous year, especially notable successes (for which management can take credit) and problems (which can be attributed to unforeseeable circumstances). In addition, there is often a preview of challenges to be met and/or steps management will take to assure the company a brighter future. This statement tells you what the firm wants people to think about it and is a good source for strategic questions about the firm, the industry and external events.

  The initial pages of the annual report also tend to give a summary of key data, for example gross revenue, net profit, number of employees. These are figures you should know. They can be a rich source for "how" and "why" questions.

  The end of an annual report provides pages of detailed financial statements. For most interviews, this information isn't needed.

  In the middle of the annual report you are likely to find a narrative about the company's products, employees, location, etc. This narrative can be a valuable source of questions.

Think about the narrative's message. If it is presenting the company's products or services, you have a source for questions about product development, market niches, client/customer preference, etc. Perhaps the narrative focuses on the firm's employees. This provides you a source for questions about corporate structure, employee relations, channels of communication, and work culture.

FIRM'S PROMOTIONAL LITERATURE

Many firm's produce promotional literature. The goal is usually to attract customers for their product or service, although sometimes the goal is public relations. In either case, promotional literature can be a great source of questions about products, clients and strategy. Sometimes there are press releases which usually promote the company's achievements. Asking about a recent event, referenced to the firm's own sources, shows that you are already thinking like a company professional.

The very nature of this material means that it is public and should be yours for the asking. Typically, you can access promotional material through a firm's public relations or shareholder relations office. Don't be reluctant to say that you want this information to prepare for your job interview. The fact that you might join the firm provides an extra reason to expedite the material to you.

TRADE PUBLICATIONS

Every profession seems to have at least one periodical which focuses on issues of significance to people in the field. For example if you are in the coal business, you would be reading *Coal Weekly* and *Coal Industry.* In addition you would probably keep up with publications like *Energy Monthly*. If you were interviewing for a job in the coal industry, you should ask at least one question which follows from what you read in these publications. Your purpose is to show that you are already "one of the gang".

Most trade publications are readily available in the periodical or reference section of a nearby library. If not, try to order at least one copy from the publisher or trade association which produces the periodical you need. Your librarian and the *Business Periodicals Index* should help you identify the relevant addresses.

BUSINESS PUBLICATIONS

At a minimum, keep up with **Business Week**. Read the whole issue. Articles on specific firms, industries, products, economics and international events are all good sources for questions. You probably can't keep up with everything, but it can be worth your time to look through recent issues of *Fortune* to see if it is carrying a major article on your firm or industry. Similarly, a daily review of the *Wall Street Journal* can be helpful.

GENERAL PRESS

The general press i.e. daily newspapers, can be useful in two ways.

- You should be keeping up with the news about events in the U.S. and abroad. It is hard to be a successful professional and be ignorant about the world, in general.

- Many papers print a business section. In a smaller community, this section may give major coverage even to a small firm if it is local. *The New York Times* is fine, but don't neglect the local press.

REFERENCE BOOKS

Most libraries carry reference books which can give you some key information upon which to build a good question. You might start with the following directories:

- *Standard & Poor's Industry Surveys* (S&P Corporation).
- *U.S. Industrial Outlook* (U.S. Department of Commerce).

These sources will give you an overview of an entire industry, including a ranking of the main competitors.

Each industry is covered succinctly, so your reading will be more intensive than extensive. This material should promote questions about market share, products, consumer/customer tastes performance compared to competitors and similar issues.

"How" and "Why"

"How" and "Why" are good questioning words to have in mind when you are reading material about the firm. Let's say that you read a statement like this in the firm's annual report:

"At Thisco, we continue to devote five percent of our after-tax income to basic research."

You can start to ask questions about the sentence which may help you form questions for your interview. For example:

- Why did they decide to invest in basic, as distinct from applied, research?

- How does Thisco's approach compare to the rest of the industry?

- How does Thisco apply its research to products it markets?

WHAT ABOUT THE JOB ITSELF

So far, we have identified sources which will help you ask good questions about the firm, the industry and external influences. What about the job itself?

If there is a **job description**, it should tell you what skills you need and may indicate the position's purpose or goals. On that basis alone you could ask about how skills would be utilized and how they contribute to company goals.

If you are a recent college graduate, the firm's **recruiting literature** will often indicate why people love their job. For example, you may be shown a picture of a recent hire with the caption "I love working at Thisco. The team work is stimulating and the demands on my analytical skills are a challenge". The picture could prompt you to ask about how teams function and how analytical skills are applied.

A useful reference book, especially for entry level jobs, is the **Occupational Outlook Handbook.** It provides brief summaries for hundreds of occupations. Usually included are a few paragraphs about the skills needed to succeed in that field. You could view that information as a generic job description.

NETWORKING

Whether your job is entry level or relatively senior, a terrific source of information is people who do a similar job or work for the company where you are interviewing. Asking people like these for advice and assistance is part of a process commonly called networking. Let's take a brief look at networking as a means to help you ask good questions.

WHO IS YOUR SOURCE?

A good source is people you know who work for your target company, a competitor, a customer or a supplier. These people can give you insights about the prospective employer from their varying perspectives. Someone who holds a job like the one you want to have can share with you his/her perceptions of the job. He or she may also provide an opportunity to test some of your questions in a safe environment.

If you don't already know people like these, how can you find them?

One good source is trade associations. Most professions are organized in associations which probably have a state or even local chapter near you. *The Encyclopedia of Associations* should help you identify the group. Acquire the local membership list; if you can, join the organization. People in a profession tend to be amendable to assisting with advice. It is considered a professional courtesy. Besides, some day they might be **coming to you** for help.

Use your family and friends to make contact with a helpful professional. Your sister doesn't have to be in your desired field to help. She may have co-workers, friends, in-laws, neighbors who can put you in touch with a good information source.

WHAT TO ASK

You could ask almost anything about the other person's job, company, industry or about external factors which might affect them. Here are some possible questions:

Q. *Would you want your son or daughter to go into this field? Why or why not?*

Q. *What attributes do you have that help you do your job well?*

Q. *What is your perception of Prospectiveco. Do they have a good reputation in terms of ethical conduct? Is the firm well managed? Will that firm still be a serious competitor in five years?*

Q. *Is your firm managed along similar lines as Prospectiveco?*

Q. *What is the most serious challenge this industry will face in the next five or ten years?*

Q. *Is this an industry where global competition is a serious factor?*

Five No-No's of Networking

There are five "don'ts" for good networking.

- **Don't Be Shy**: Asking for help is the best way to get it.

- **Don't Be Greedy**: Be mindful of the limited time each contact has.

- **Don't Feel Like a Beggar**: On the other hand, there is nothing sleazy or demeaning to be looking for career assistance. Some day, you may be able to return the favor.

- **Don't Lose Perspective**: Be realistic and patient. Every contact can be a step towards achieving your goal. No contact is the magic pill to solve your problems

- **Don't Forget Your Contacts**: Thank them by letter after your meeting. Let them know when you have landed your job.

This chapter told you how to research effectively to give your questions the greatest impact. The previous chapters gave you 101 dynamite questions to ask at your job interview. The next chapter is up to you. Let me know how your job search progresses.

You can reach me at:

Richard Fein
c/o School of Management
University of Massachusetts
Box 34960
Amherst, MA 01003-3858

INDEX

CAREER
RESOURCES

Contact Impact Publications to receive a free copy of their latest comprehensive and annotated catalog of career resources (hundreds of books, directories, subscriptions, training programs, audiocassettes, videos, computer software programs, multimedia, and CD-ROM).

The following career resources are available directly from Impact Publications. Complete the following form or list the titles, include shipping (see the formula at the end), enclose payment, and send your order to:

IMPACT PUBLICATIONS
9104-N Manassas Drive
Manassas Park, VA 22111-5211
Tel. 703/361-7300 or Fax 703/335-9486

Orders from individuals must be prepaid by check, moneyorder, Visa, MasterCard, or American Express number. We accept telephone and fax orders with a credit card number.

Qty.	TITLES	Price	TOTAL

INTERVIEWS & SALARY NEGOTIATIONS

Qty.	TITLES	Price	TOTAL
___	60 Seconds and You're Hired!	$ 9.95	___
___	101 Questions to Ask At Your Job Interview	$14.95	___
___	Conquer Interview Objections	$10.95	___
___	Dynamite Answers to Interview Questions	$11.95	___
___	Dynamite Salary Negotiation	$12.95	___
___	Interview for Success	$13.95	___
___	Interview Power	$12.95	___
___	Naked At the Interview	$10.95	___

___ Perfect Interview $17.95 ___
___ Power Interviews $12.95 ___
___ Sweaty Palms $8.95 ___

DRESS, APPEARANCE, IMAGE

___ 110 Mistakes Working Women Make/Dressing Smart $9.95 ___
___ John Molloy's New Dress for Success $10.95 ___
___ Red Socks Don't Work! (Men's Clothing) $14.95 ___

RESUMES, LETTERS, & NETWORKING

___ Dynamite Cover Letters $11.95 ___
___ Dynamite Resumes $11.95 ___
___ Electronic Resumes for the New Job Market $11.95 ___
___ Great Connections $11.95 ___
___ High Impact Resumes and Letters $14.95 ___
___ How to Work a Room $9.95 ___
___ Job Search Letters That Get Results $15.95 ___
___ New Network Your Way to Job and Career Success $15.95 ___

JOB SEARCH STRATEGIES AND TACTICS

___ Change Your Job, Change Your Life $15.95 ___
___ Complete Job Finder's Guide to the 90's $13.95 ___
___ Dynamite Tele-Search $12.95 ___
___ Five Secrets to Finding a Job $12.95 ___
___ How to Get Interviews From Classified Job Ads $14.95 ___
___ How to Succeed Without a Career Path $13.95 ___
___ Rites of Passage at $100,000+ $29.95 ___
___ Ultimate Job Source CD-ROM $49.95 ___
___ What Color Is Your Parachute? $14.95· ___

BEST JOBS AND EMPLOYERS FOR THE 90's

___ 100 Best Companies to Work for in America $27.95 ___
___ 100 Best Jobs for the 1990s and Beyond $19.95 ___
___ 101 Careers $14.95 ___
___ 150 Companies for Liberal Arts Graduates $12.95 ___
___ Adams Jobs Almanac 1996 $15.00 ___
___ American Almanac of Jobs and Salaries $17.00 ___
___ America's Fastest Growing Employers $15.95 ___
___ Best Jobs for the 1990s and Into the 21st Century $19.95 ___
___ Careers Encyclopedia $39.95 ___
___ Companies That Care $12.95 ___
___ Great Place to Work $9.95 ___
___ Hoover's Guide to Computer Companies (with disk) $34.95 ___
___ Hoover's Masterlist of 2,500 of America's
      Largest and Fastest Growing Employers (with disk) $19.95 ___
___ Job Seeker's Guide to 1000 Top Employers $22.95 ___
___ Jobs 1996 $15.00 ___
___ Jobs Rated Almanac $16.95 ___

___ New Emerging Careers $14.95 _____
___ Quantum Companies $21.95 _____
___ Top Professions $10.95 _____

ALTERNATIVE JOBS AND CAREERS

___ Advertising Career Directory $17.95 _____
___ Business and Finance Career Directory $17.95 _____
___ But What If I Don't Want to Go to College? $10.95 _____
___ Career Opportunities in Art $29.95 _____
___ Career Opportunities in Music Industry $29.95 _____
___ Career Opportunities in the Sports Industry $29.95 _____
___ Career Opportunities in Television, Cable, and Video $29.95 _____
___ Career Opportunities in Theater and Performing Arts $29.95 _____
___ Career Opportunities in Writing $29.95 _____
___ Careers for Animal Lovers $12.95 _____
___ Careers for Bookworms $12.95 _____
___ Careers for Computer Buffs $12.95 _____
___ Careers for Craft People $12.95 _____
___ Careers for Culture Lovers $12.95 _____
___ Careers for Environmental Types $12.95 _____
___ Careers for Foreign Language Aficionados $12.95 _____
___ Careers for Good Samaritans $12.95 _____
___ Careers for Gourmets $12.95 _____
___ Careers for History Buffs $12.95 _____
___ Careers for Kids at Heart $12.95 _____
___ Careers for Nature Lovers $12.95 _____
___ Careers for Night Owls $12.95 _____
___ Careers for Number Crunchers $12.95 _____
___ Careers for Shutterbugs $12.95 _____
___ Careers for Sports Nuts $12.95 _____
___ Careers for Travel Buffs $12.95 _____
___ Careers in Accounting $16.95 _____
___ Careers in Advertising $16.95 _____
___ Careers in Business $16.95 _____
___ Careers in Child Care $16.95 _____
___ Careers in Communications $16.95 _____
___ Careers in Computers $16.95 _____
___ Careers in Education $16.95 _____
___ Careers in Engineering $16.95 _____
___ Careers in Finance $16.95 _____
___ Careers in Government $16.95 _____
___ Careers in Health Care $16.95 _____
___ Careers in High Tech $16.95 _____
___ Careers in Journalism $16.95 _____
___ Careers in Law $16.95 _____
___ Careers in Marketing $16.95 _____
___ Careers in Medicine $16.95 _____
___ Careers in Science $16.95 _____
___ Careers in Social and Rehabilitation Services $16.95 _____
___ Environmental Career Directory $17.95 _____
___ Job Opps in Business $19.95 _____
___ Job Opps in Engineering and Technology $19.95 _____

___ Job Opps in Health Care $19.95 _____
___ Jobs for People Who Love Computers and the
      the Information Highway $13.95 _____
___ Jobs for People Who Love Hotels, Resorts,
      and Cruise Ships $13.95 _____
___ Jobs for People Who Love Health Care and Nursing $13.95 _____
___ Jobs for People Who Love to Work From Home $13.95 _____
___ Jobs for People Who Love Travel $15.95 _____
___ Marketing and Sales Career Directory $17.95 _____
___ Opportunities in Advertising $13.95 _____
___ Opportunities in Airline Careers $13.95 _____
___ Opportunities in Banking $13.95 _____
___ Opportunities in Broadcasting $13.95 _____
___ Opportunities in Business Management $13.95 _____
___ Opportunities in Child Care $13.95 _____
___ Opportunities in Craft Careers $13.95 _____
___ Opportunities in Electrical Trades $13.95 _____
___ Opportunities in Eye Care $13.95 _____
___ Opportunities in Gerontology $13.95 _____
___ Opportunities in Interior Design $13.95 _____
___ Opportunities in Laser Technology $13.95 _____
___ Opportunities in Microelectronics $13.95 _____
___ Opportunities in Nonprofit Organizations $13.95 _____
___ Opportunities in Optometry $13.95 _____
___ Opportunities in Pharmacy $13.95 _____
___ Opportunities in Psychology $13.95 _____
___ Opportunities in Public Relations $13.95 _____
___ Opportunities in Robotics $13.95 _____
___ Opportunities in Sports and Athletics $13.95 _____
___ Opportunities in Sports Medicine $13.95 _____
___ Opportunities in Telecommunications $13.95 _____
___ Opportunities in Transportation $13.95 _____
___ Opportunities in Trucking $13.95 _____
___ Opportunities in Waste Management $13.95 _____
___ Outdoor Careers $14.95 _____
___ Radio and Television Career Directory $17.95 _____
___ Travel and Hospitality Career Directory $17.95 _____

KEY DIRECTORIES

___ American Salaries and Wages Survey $115.00 _____
___ Career Training Sourcebook $24.95 _____
___ Careers Encyclopedia $39.95 _____
___ Dictionary of Occupational Titles $39.95 _____
___ Directory of Executive Recruiters $44.95 _____
___ Encyclopedia of Associations $1,160.00 _____
___ Encyclopedia of Careers & Vocational Guidance $129.95 _____
___ Hoover's American Business $29.95 _____
___ Hoover's World Business $27.95 _____
___ Internships 1996 $21.95 _____
___ Job Bank Guide to Employment Services $149.95 _____
___ Job Hunter's Sourcebook $69.95 _____
___ Moving and Relocation Directory $179.95 _____

___ National Fax Directory $99.00   _____
___ National Job Bank $249.95   _____
___ National Trade and Professional Associations $79.95   _____
___ Occupational Outlook Handbook $21.95   _____
___ Personnel Executives Contactbook $149.00   _____
___ Professional Careers Sourcebook $89.95   _____
___ Vocational Careers Sourcebook $79.95   _____

TELEPHONE AND JOB HOTLINE DIRECTORIES

___ Directory of Executive Recruiters $44.95   _____
___ Government Directory of Addresses
    and Telephone Numbers $149.95   _____
___ Job Hotlines USA $24.95   _____
___ Job Hunter's Yellow Pages $59.00   _____
___ National Directory of Addresses and
    Telephone Numbers $99.95   _____

JOB VACANCY SOURCEBOOKS

___ Government Job Finder $16.95   _____
___ Non-Profit's Job Finder $16.95   _____
___ Professional's Private Sector Job Finder $18.95   _____

ELECTRONIC JOB SEARCH RESOURCES

___ Electronic Job Search Revolution $12.95   _____
___ Electronic Resume Revolution $12.95   _____
___ Electronic Resumes for the New Job Market $11.95   _____
___ Hook Up, Get Hired $12.95   _____
___ The Job-Seeker's Guide to On-Line Resources $14.95   _____
___ On-Line Job Search Companion $14.95   _____
___ Using the Internet in Your Job Search $16.95   _____

CITY AND STATE JOB FINDERS (Adams Media's Job Banks)

___ Atlanta $15.95   _____
___ Boston $15.95   _____
___ Chicago $15.95   _____
___ Dallas/Fort Worth $15.95   _____
___ Denver $15.95   _____
___ Florida $15.95   _____
___ Houston $15.95   _____
___ Los Angeles $15.95   _____
___ Minneapolis $15.95   _____
___ New York $15.95   _____
___ Philadelphia $15.95   _____
___ San Francisco $15.95   _____
___ Seattle $15.95   _____
___ Washington, DC $15.95   _____

CITY AND STATE JOB FINDERS (Surrey Books)

___ Atlanta	$15.95	_____
___ Boston	$15.95	_____
___ Dallas/Fort Worth	$15.95	_____
___ Houston	$15.95	_____
___ New York	$15.95	_____
___ San Francisco	$15.95	_____
___ Seattle and Portland	$15.95	_____
___ Southern California	$15.95	_____
___ Washington, DC	$15.95	_____

INTERNATIONAL, OVERSEAS, AND TRAVEL JOBS

___ Almanac of International Jobs and Careers	$19.95	_____
___ Complete Guide to International Jobs & Careers	$13.95	_____
___ Guide to Careers in World Affairs	$14.95	_____
___ How to Get a Job in Europe	$17.95	_____
___ How to Get a Job in the Pacific Rim	$17.95	_____
___ Jobs for People Who Love Travel	$15.95	_____
___ Jobs in Russia and the Newly Independent States	$15.95	_____
___ Jobs Worldwide	$17.95	_____

PUBLIC-ORIENTED CAREERS

___ Complete Guide to Public Employment	$19.95	_____
___ Directory of Federal Jobs and Employers	$21.95	_____
___ Federal Applications That Get Results	$23.95	_____
___ Federal Jobs in Computers	$14.95	_____
___ Federal Jobs in Finance and Accounting	$14.95	_____
___ Federal Jobs in Law Enforcement	$14.95	_____
___ Federal Jobs in Nursing and Health Sciences	$14.95	_____
___ Federal Jobs in Office Administration	$14.95	_____
___ Federal Jobs in Secret Operations	$14.95	_____
___ Find a Federal Job Fast!	$13.95	_____
___ Government Job Finder	$16.95	_____
___ Jobs and Careers With Nonprofit Organizations	$15.95	_____

JOB LISTINGS & VACANCY ANNOUNCEMENTS

___ Executive Recruiter News	$157.00	_____
___ Federal Career Opportunities (6 biweekly issues)	$39.00	_____
___ International Employment Gazette (6 biweekly issues)	$35.00	_____

SKILLS, TESTING, SELF-ASSESSMENT

___ Discover the Best Jobs for You	$11.95	_____
___ Do What You Are	$15.95	_____
___ Do What You Love, the Money Will Follow	$11.95	_____
___ I Could Do Anything If I Only Know What It Was	$19.95	_____
___ Where Do I Go With the Rest of My Life?	$11.95	_____
___ Wishcraft	$11.95	_____

MILITARY

___ From Air Force Blue to Corporate Gray	$17.95 ___
___ From Army Green to Corporate Gray	$15.95 ___
___ From Navy Blue to Corporate Gray	$17.95 ___
___ Job Search: Marketing Your Military Experience	$16.95 ___
___ Resumes and Cover Letters for Transitioning Military Personnel	$17.95 ___

WOMEN AND SPOUSES

___ Doing It All Isn't Everything	$19.95 ___
___ New Relocating Spouse's Guide to Employment	$14.95 ___
___ Resumes for Re-Entry: A Handbook for Women	$10.95 ___
___ Survival Guide for Women	$16.95 ___

MINORITIES AND DISABLED

___ Best Companies for Minorities	$12.00 ___
___ Big Book of Minority Opportunities	$39.95 ___
___ Job Strategies for People With Disabilities	$14.95 ___
___ Minority Organizations	$49.95 ___

ENTREPRENEURSHIP AND SELF-EMPLOYMENT

___ 101 Best Businesses to Start	$15.00 ___
___ Best Home-Based Businesses for the 90s	$12.95 ___
___ Entrepreneur's Guide to Starting a Successful Business	$16.95 ___

VIDEOS

___ Dialing for Jobs	$139.00 ___
___ Directing Your Successful Job Search	$99.95 ___
___ Find the Job You Want...and Get It!	$229.95 ___
___ Interview Power	$29..95 ___
___ JobSearch—The Inside Track	$1295.00 ___
___ Looking Ahead	$129.95 ___
___ Winning At Job Hunting in the 90s	$89.95 ___

COMPUTER SOFTWARE PROGRAMS (IBM or Compatibles)

___ Cambridge Career Counseling System	$349.00 ___
___ INSTANT Job Hunting Letters	$39.95 ___
___ JobHunt for Window®	$59.95 ___
___ Resumemaker With Career Planning	$49.95 ___
___ You're Hired!	$59.95 ___

CD-ROM

___ America's Top Jobs	$295.00 ___
___ CD-ROM Version of the Occupational Outlook Handbook	$399.00 ___

___ Electronic Guide for Occupational Exploration	$295.00	_____
___ Encyclopedia of Careers and Vocational Guidance	$199.95	_____
___ Interview Skills of the Future	$199.00	_____
___ Job Search Skills of the 21st Century	$199.00	_____
___ Multimedia Career Center	$385.00	_____
___ Occupational Outlook On CD-ROM	$29.95	_____
___ Resume Revolution	$99.00	_____
___ Tech Prep Careers for the Future	$349.00	_____
___ Ultimate Job Source (Individual Version)	$49.95	_____
___ Ultimate Job Source (Professional Version with DOT)	$149.95	_____

SUBTOTAL _____

Virginia residents add 4½% sales tax _____

POSTAGE/HANDLING ($4 for first
product and $1 for each additional) $4.00

Number of additional titles x $1.00 ---------- _____

TOTAL ENCLOSED ----------------- _____

NAME _____

ADDRESS _____

_____

_____

❑ I enclose check/moneyorder for $ _____ made payable to
IMPACT PUBLICATIONS.

❑ Please charge $ _____ to my credit card:

Card # _____

Expiration date: _____/_____

Signature _____

SEND TO: **IMPACT PUBLICATIONS**, 9104-N Manassas Drive,
Manassas Park, VA 22111-5211, Tel. 703/361-7300 or
Fax 703/335-9486